Marilyn

HER LIFE IN HER OWN WORDS

Marilyn

HER LIFE IN HER OWN WORDS

MARILYN MONROE'S
REVEALING LAST WORDS
AND PHOTOGRAPHS

GEORGE BARRIS

Citadel Press
Kensington Publishing Corp.
www.kensingtonbooks.com

CITADEL PRESS books are published by

Kensington Publishing Corp.
850 Third Avenue
New York, NY 10022

All Kensington titles, imprints, and distributed lines are available at special quantity
discounts for bulk purchases for sales promotions, premiums, fund-raising, educational,
or institutional use. Special book excerpts or customized printings can also be created
to fit specific needs. For details, write or phone the office of the Kensington special
sales manager: Kensington Publishing Corp., 850 Third Avenue, New York, NY 10022,
attn: Special Sales Department, phone 1-800-221-2647.

First Citadel Press printing: April 2001
First paperback printing: June 2003

10   9   8   7   6   5   4   3

Printed in the United States of America

Library of Congress Cataloging-in-Publication Data

Monroe, Marilyn, 1926–1962.
    Marilyn—her life in her own words : Marilyn Monroe's revealing
last words and photographs / by George Barris.
        p.   cm.
    ISBN 0–8065–2453–7
    1. Monroe, Marilyn, 1926–1962—Interviews. 2. Monroe Marilyn,
1926–1962—Portraits. I. Barris, George. II. Title
PN2287.M69A5   1995
791.43'028'092—dc20
                                                                                        95-19254
                                                                                        CIP

To Marilyn—Norma Jeane,
who became a legend in her lifetime.
For all the joy and happiness you brought to a troubled world.
We love you, we miss you. Thanks for your friendship.

Contents

There's always two sides to a story.

—MARILYN

Introduction

I HAD ALWAYS WANTED TO WORK ON A BOOK with Marilyn Monroe, from the first time I met her on a freelance photographic assignment back in September 1954. At that time she was in New York City on location for *The Seven Year Itch*. I initially conceived of the book as an ongoing series of my photographs of her as she went through her daily activities over the next several years, accompanied by her words as I interviewed her. Unfortunately such a book was never to be, but I think the one you are reading now gives new life to Marilyn.

Earlier in 1954, I had suggested to one of my editors, the late Donald Feitel of the Metro Group, that I produce a picture-text story. Since Marilyn had become so popular, her fans and the public couldn't read enough about her, especially about the candid, off-guard moments in her life. Feitel agreed and suggested I take as many pictures of her as I could manage.

When I first caught sight of Marilyn, she was leaning out the window of a brownstone on fashionable 61st Street on the East Side of Manhattan, posing for a film scene. Actually my first glimpse was of her behind. When I took some photos of that now-famous backside, the sound of the camera's shutter surprised her. She quickly turned around, spotted me, and smiled. I took a dozen more pictures, we both laughed, and the ice was completely broken. She certainly had a sense of humor. I subsequently followed Marilyn around for days, interviewing her and taking photos. She was great to work with.

What I particularly liked about Marilyn was that she didn't act like a movie star. She was down to earth. Although she was then twenty-eight, she looked and acted like a teenager. Sure, she was beautiful and sexy, but there was an almost childlike innocence about her. I was most impressed that Marilyn was always polite and friendly to everyone on the set. She was no phony or snob.

Amazing as it seems, in the few days I worked with her we became friends. We discovered that we'd been born under the same sign: Gemini. Marilyn's birthday was June 1; mine June 14. We liked the same things, and she was easy to talk to. I told her I'd like to work with her on a book about her life. She thought about it for a while; then her eyes opened wide, she smiled and answered, "Why not? Let's do it someday."

But it wasn't until 1962 that we finally got around to seriously thinking about putting our book together. She had been busy making film after film and had become the international star I knew she was meant to be. I was busy traveling the world doing my stories. And though we had not seen each other, we had kept in touch—thanks to the telephone.

In May 1962 I was on assignment for *Cosmopolitan* magazine for a cover story on Elizabeth Taylor, who was then filming *Cleopatra* in Rome. Elizabeth was the first actress to receive a million dollars, plus expenses, for appearing in a film. The film shoot had begun in England, where Liz became ill and nearly died. Twentieth Century-Fox, the same studio that then employed Marilyn, had moved the production to Rome, where the warm climate better suited Elizabeth. There she could recuperate from a recent operation and resume filming. Not only was the star sick, but the entire production was in serious trouble. The studio was going bankrupt because of the film's enormous expenses. There was no completed script; writers were writing scenes the same day they were filmed. Richard Burton was having an affair with Taylor while she was married to singer Eddie Fisher. Fisher had no idea how to put a stop to his wife's affair. What a fiasco—I couldn't wait to get back to New York.

Once back in the City, I had lunch with Bob Atherton, the editor of *Cosmopolitan*. As a photojournalist my livelihood usually depended on suggesting salable magazine stories to the editors I freelanced for. My friend Marilyn Monroe was making news. She was starting her thirtieth film, which would be her last for Twentieth Century-Fox under her old contract. It was time I did a major story on her. The idea I presented to the *Cosmopolitan* editor: What was Marilyn's future now that she was turning thirty-six? The title of the film she was working on, *Something's Got to Give,* could well apply to her career. Could she at thirty-six continue to play sexy, beautiful young women?

Atherton loved the idea. We agreed that it would make a cover and eight to ten pages in the magazine. The idea so excited us both that we didn't even finish our lunch. He asked me how soon I could leave for Hollywood, where the film was already in production at the Fox studios. I told him I could leave immediately.

When I got to Hollywood, I checked into the Sunset Tower apartments on the Sunset Strip. After a good night's sleep, a studio limousine took me the next morning to the Fox studio and Stage 14, where Marilyn was filming. Would she be glad to see me? Would she even remember me by sight? Many big stars meet so many people they have trouble remembering who they were introduced to the previous day—and we hadn't seen each other for a few years.

When I entered Stage 14, I spotted Marilyn right away and walked over. Her back was to me, so I tapped her on the shoulder. "Hi. Remember me?"

She turned around, smiled, and, with a big hug, said, "It's been a long time. What's the occasion?"

"Well," I replied, "since today is June first, I thought I'd fly out from New York to see my ol' friend—note I said *ol',* not *old."*

She laughed as I hugged her again and said, "Happy-happy, and may you have only happy ones." I told her about the *Cosmo* story; she loved it.

"Maybe, Marilyn," I suggested, "it's time we did the book we talked about all these years."

She laughed. "Maybe the time is right now. Why not?" George Cukor called for her to appear on the set. Marilyn asked me to stick around—we could talk about the book, and other things, later.

Marilyn seemed excited about the film. Her leading man was Dean Martin, whom she had always wanted to work with, and she had gotten good parts for two of her friends. Both were comedians—Phil Silvers, the TV star of the old *Sergeant Bilko* show, and Wally Cox, who had played Mr. Peepers on TV years before. Also in the film was her friend Cyd Charisse, the dancer and wife of actor-singer Tony Martin.

At five thirty that Friday afternoon, Marilyn had finished her scene. It was time for her to call it a day. Then someone shouted "Happy birthday, Marilyn!" One of the crew wheeled out a huge birthday cake. It had white frosting with a sexy sketch of Marilyn in a bikini and HAPPY BIRTHDAY MARILYN written in huge letters—topped with July Fourth sparklers shooting tiny stars. And of course there was Marilyn's champagne, Dom Perignon.

The Fox film crew and cast had remembered Marilyn on her birthday, and this brought tears of joy to the excited actress. She motioned to me to come over and help her cut the enormous cake. The photographers took pictures of us together while everyone was singing "Happy birthday, dear Marilyn / We all love you, and may all your wishes come true." I had never seen a happier Marilyn.

By six thirty, Marilyn had passed out slices of the cake and glasses of champagne to everyone. She waved a goodbye, turned to me, and said, "Let's get together Monday morning early on the set, around eight."

Monday, June 4, arrived, and I was on the set early—but there was no Marilyn. In fact, Marilyn did not show up for work all week. She sent word that she was sick at home with a virus, a high temperature, sore throat, and stomach pains.

With Marilyn out sick all week, the Fox executives began to panic. They had depended on Marilyn's movie to rescue the studio from its impending bankruptcy. They did not want to believe that she was sick. They even sent the studio doctor to check her out, and when he reported back on her illness, they still refused to believe she was too sick to work.

The publicity department released stories to the press (under studio executives' orders) that Marilyn was out to ruin Fox. They implied that she did not care about the huge staff of workers on the film who were

now unemployed because she refused to show up for work. The studio brass became so desperate that on Friday, June 8, they ordered a story released to the press stating they were going to sue Marilyn for half a million dollars for delaying production. They would also replace her with another actress, and this would be the end of Marilyn's career.

When Marilyn heard, she was shocked. She couldn't believe what the studio was doing to her. She said, "It's all right when the Fox executives get sick. They can stay home. But Marilyn, what right has she to get sick? Those bastards, how could they do this to me, after all the millions I've made for that studio?" Finally the Fox executives decided to suspend Marilyn and shelve *Something's Got to Give* until further notice.

That very weekend Marilyn and I began working on our *Cosmopolitan* and book projects. This would keep us busy, and I hoped it would keep Marilyn from thinking about her problems with the studio. She had asked me to shop for clothes for her to wear in the photographs, and I also had to locate a house for our sessions, since Marilyn's was unfurnished. She was still waiting for the arrival of furniture she had bought in Mexico some time ago.

On my shopping spree for Marilyn, I went to two of her favorite stores, Jaks on Wilshire Boulevard in Beverly Hills, and Saks Fifth Avenue. At Jaks I bought her some beautiful slacks and decorative Emilio Pucci sport shirts. Then off to Saks for a bulky sweater, terry-cloth three-quarter hooded beach jacket, a blanket, a large towel for those peek-a-boo beach shots, and a sexy bikini. I did not buy Marilyn any undergarments—she never wore them.

My friend Tim Leimert was willing to let us use his house, located in the North Hollywood Hills, providing I would introduce him to Marilyn. Tim's home was beautifully furnished with expensive paintings and sculpture. He also had a huge garden and patio. Only a swimming pool was missing—but Marilyn's house had one—so the high quality of our backgrounds was assured. Tim promised not to hang around while I interviewed and photographed Marilyn.

When Marilyn and I got to Tim's house, I introduced him and his maid, Louise, to Marilyn. Louise became so nervous when Marilyn shook her hand that she fluttered and stuttered, saying, "Is that really you? No one will believe me when I say I met and shook hands with Marilyn Monroe. I can hardly believe it myself. Is that really you?"

Marilyn, laughing, replied, "Sometimes I can hardly believe it, too." Tim kept his word, and soon afterward, accompanied by the still flustered Louise, he left his house.

So, for the weeks from June 9 until July 18, I was busy working with Marilyn. I had taken a group of indoor and outdoor shots, including a series at Santa Monica beach, and I had interviewed Marilyn at length for our *Cosmo* story and for our book. She was wonderful to work with the entire time; she never looked more beautiful, nor was she ever so talkative. Our book project was more important than ever to her after all those lies the Fox studio had handed out to the press. The media didn't even have the common courtesy to tell her side of the story.

I returned to New York July 20 to work on our projects and was spending the weekend in the country with my family. On Sunday I drove my brother-in-law to the local general store. I was waiting outside in the car when my brother-in-law came running out, shouting to me that he'd just heard on the radio that Marilyn Monroe was dead, at the age of thirty-six.

After Marilyn's death, the press was constantly hounding me for interviews about Marilyn, especially since I had seen and spoken with her so shortly before her death. To escape the pressure I fled to Paris, where I remained for over twenty years. I married a French actress, Sylvie Constantine, and we have two lovely daughters, Caroline and Stephanie. In 1982 I moved back to the United States with my family, and we settled in the Los Angeles area. My family was eager to see where Marilyn was interred, so I took them to visit her crypt, where I introduced them to

Marilyn. We all said a prayer for her—she had become part of our lives.

Why have I waited all these years before deciding to have this book published? I was in a state of shock after Marilyn died. Of course I wanted to keep our last conversations and many of her photos private. But now that I have grown older and wiser, I realize that Marilyn belongs to the public and her millions of fans.

She was in great spirits in her final days. She was full of life and couldn't wait to get started on the next phase of her career. Although none of her husbands or friends seemed to bring her the happiness she was seeking, I will never believe that she took her own life. It will always be my conviction that she was murdered. But no matter how she died, we all lost her too soon. I hope this book brings you pleasure, as she did.

—GEORGE BARRIS

Acknowledgments

I WISH TO THANK MY WIFE, Sylvie, my daughter Caroline—and especially my daughter Stephanie, for her untiring and loyal devotion to this book. She has guided me in the use of her Macintosh computer, and I'll never use my electronic typewriter again.

My thanks to my editor, Hillel Black, my publisher, Steven Schragis, and my loyal agent, George J. Wieser, for their support, too. I'm grateful for the work of Louise Fili and of Jim Davis's Hallas Photo Laboratory, particularly that of Donna, Stewart, and Birgit, and for the time and effort of Carol Publishing Group staff members Diane Chin, Anne Ricigliano, and Margaret Wolf. And thanks to Eastman Kodak, Nikon, and Rollei-flex.

Marilyn

HER LIFE IN HER OWN WORDS

1

"LIES, LIES, LIES"

ies, lies, lies, nothing but lies. Everything they've been saying about me is lies. You are the first one I'm telling it to. I'll tell you all about my childhood, career, marriages, and divorces—but most important, what I want most out of life.

I was born according to the records (and my birth certificate) Norma Jeane Mortenson, approximately nine thirty in the morning on June 1, 1926, at Los Angeles General Hospital [now County University of Southern California Medical Center].

Yes, it's true I was born an illegitimate child. I also spent a part of my childhood in and out of foster homes—and to top it off I landed in an orphanage [from the time] I was nine to eleven, even though my mother was still alive. My mother? Sure I had a mother, doesn't everyone have a mother? About my father? Well, I guess that's what caused my mother to have problems in life. No, I never got to know my father.

You know, my mother was a very attractive woman when she was young, but she used to say the beauty in the family was her mother.

My grandmother was something—all the boys were after her. She was from Dublin, Ireland, you know, where all the girls are pretty. Her family name was Hogan. My grandfather? He came from Scotland and I remember, as strange as it seemed, she spoke with a slight Scottish brogue. I remember it sounded nice, sort of musical. My father's father, my grandfather, I was told, was born in Haugesund, Norway. He and my grandmother met in Los Angeles after the First World War.

My mother once told me my father died in an accident when I was quite young. My father wasn't married to my mother when I was born. In fact, he left my mother when

GEORGE BARRIS: Marilyn always seemed determined to talk to me about her childhood. We would be discussing a subject of current interest to her, and she would somehow bring up an incident from her bygone days.

Even when she talked about the future, she drifted back to the past. I think she was a dreamer and nostalgic about those early days. She was always honest in our conversations, and if she didn't want to discuss a part of her life in detail, she would politely smile and give me a brief answer.

Did Marilyn always tell me the truth? I believe so, even though, being an accomplished actress, she may have dramatized some events and added a bit of color to them—still the facts were there. Her eyes would tell me she was truthful, while her voice revealed the drama, so that I could feel the pain or joy she had gone through. Her way of rendering a story helped me understand her better. She was a person of passion and great love, even when things were not going well for her.

Sometimes I felt a sadness watching her, a beautiful girl who had achieved the impossible, the dream of all beautiful, talented girls—fame as an actress on the silver screen. I could see a sadness in her eyes; she had learned to smile, laugh, and clown,

he heard from her that I was on the way. His name: Stanley Gifford. I was their love child. He told my mother that she should be glad she was married to Ed Mortenson—at least she could give the baby his name. Stanley Gifford offered my mother money, but she refused. She was willing to get a divorce and marry him, but he wouldn't do the right thing by her—even if she divorced her husband.

I guess that's what broke her heart—you know what I mean. When you love a man and tell him you're going to have his child and he runs out on you, it's something a woman never gets over. I don't think my mother did. I don't think I ever did. Yes, it's a fact, I was conceived perhaps in a moment of passion by my mother, who had always loved me—and by a father who would not recognize his obligation to a child that passion would conceive. A father in the eyes of the law, but one who would have nothing to do with his child. Even when I became a successful movie star, he still refused to acknowledge me. All I really wanted from him was to let me call him my father. But

even though her heart was breaking.

When I photographed Marilyn, I sometimes encouraged her to think about her childhood and the days when she was sweet Norma Jeane, not about Marilyn Monroe the movie star she had become. She understood instinctively what I wanted. The chemistry between us worked perfectly. It seemed to me that a magnet had drawn us together for this project, which excited us both.

During our picture-taking sessions she amazed me with her youthful vitality. Her energy seemed endless. She would run into the chilly ocean water and allow the waves to nearly knock her down—just like a kid. Then she'd laugh and tell me how much fun she was having. She said she had acted the same way as a child. It was obvious that she truly loved the ocean. As I watched her, I asked if the ocean antics brought back memories of her childhood. She laughed and replied, "Yeah."

One day at the ocean, Marilyn told me, "If the waves and undertow take me out to sea and I never come back, don't forget our book. You are the one I'm depending on to get it published. Don't forget. Promise me." I told her not to worry, that I'd never let her down. "I trust you," she replied.

All I really wanted from him was to
let me call him my father.

he wouldn't give me the satisfaction of knowing him. He didn't want the world to know I was his love child, his mistake.

You want to know something about my childhood? Well, even though I did have some horrible experiences, and one that I'll never forget, there are two memories that I cherish dearly. But I'll tell you about them a little later on. I'll tell you about my marriages, too.

2

"HOW I WISHED I HAD A DAD"

My mother, Gladys, was born in Mexico (of American parents) in 1900. The family later moved back to the Los Angeles area, where they had originally lived. Gladys had two children by her then husband, Jack Baker. Those children were kidnapped by her husband and taken to live with him in Kentucky. Gladys then married Edward Mortenson. [As I said], I was the love child of an affair she had with a divorced salesman (they both worked at the same film lab) named C. Stanley Gifford. I was that love child named Norma Jeane. My father would have nothing to do with me or my mother, and so I was baptized when I was six months old as Norma Jeane Baker by Sister Aimee Semple McPherson at the Four Square Gospel Church in Hawthorne, California.

As long as I can remember, I've always loved people. When I was a small child, my fondest memories were being around my mother and her friends. It made me feel like we were one big happy family.

Whenever Mom or her friends bought me an ice cream cone, we'd go for a walk or to the movies. I was in heaven when we went to church; I looked forward to this, even if it wasn't every week. The singing and services always excited me. I was sort of in a trance. There I was, dressed in my best clothes. Then, about noon, it was back home, where we always had a chicken lunch with our family—Mom and her friends. Then off we would go for a stroll, looking in the fancy store windows at things we couldn't afford to buy: We were dreamers.

What made me sad was seeing other kids with their moms and dads strolling around holding hands. Oh, how I wished I had a dad, too. I know Mom loved me and tried to make my days happy ones, but most days she seemed sad and lonely. I'm sure it was because there was no man in her life. No man to love her and me. No husband, no daddy. When I thought about this, it made me sad, too. I had no daddy to hug, to talk to or play with, just to love.

Mom really tried her best. She worked at the Consolidated Film Industries lab as a cutter of the negative film. It was long hours, low pay, at a boring and tedious eye-

GEORGE BARRIS: I remember Marilyn talking about the sadness her mother knew during all those years, how even her mother's lover, the man who fathered Marilyn, rejected Gladys and their love child, how painful for Marilyn it had been when she found him and tried to become his friend. Imagine her pain when he told her never to bother him.

Later on, her biggest enemy was Marilyn Monroe. Her true self was little Norma Jeane. Often she couldn't believe that little girl had become a world-famous star. Her new life was like a dream to her, and her greatest fear was that one day she would wake up and discover it was all make-believe, a rags-to-riches-back-to-rags life.

straining job. And making ends meet was just too much for her. Since she was at her job most of the time, she had to pay others to look after me. Sometimes I would get to see her only early in the morning or at night. It was enough for any mom to have a nervous breakdown. All I can remember was her being in and out of hospitals.

But I never blamed her for my having to live in other homes. If only there was a daddy there to love and care for me.

My mother was working long hours at the film lab just to make ends meet. She became very tired and nervous; life had become difficult for her. She had to be sent to the hospital for a rest when I was only five years old. That's what caused her to have a nervous breakdown. That's what caused me to spend my childhood in and out of foster homes.

Let me lean closer to you and slowly and softly tell you what happened to a sad, lonely little girl. I was living in the home of my mother's best friend. Then she remarries. All of a sudden her house became too small, and someone had to go. Guess who that someone had to be?

One day she packed my clothes in my suitcase, and off we went in her car. She drove and drove for a long time without saying where she was taking me. She never said a word when I asked her. She just kept driving, looking straight ahead.

I realized why she had kept secret for so long that her mother was alive but in a mental hospital and why she told no one about the nude calendar picture for which she posed when she was young and broke. Neither was a matter of shame for her, but she was afraid that revealing the truth might damage or even end her fabulous career. However, her religious upbringing with Aunt Ana, a churchgoing Christian Scientist, had taught her that truth would overcome anything. That is why Marilyn Monroe eventually told all. The truth saved her pride, and her career. Her fans loved her more than ever for her honesty.

We finally arrived at a three-story red-brick building. She made me carry my small suitcase as we walked up the stairs to the main entrance of the building. I noticed a sign in huge letters. Emptiness came over me; my heart began beating fast, then faster. I broke out in a cold sweat. I began to panic. I cried. I couldn't catch my breath. The sign said Los Angeles Orphans Home. Please don't let me stay here. I'm not an orphan—my mother's not dead. I'm not an orphan. It's just that she's sick in the hospital and can't take care of me. Please don't make me stay here. I cried and protested as hard as I could; I can still remember, she had to drag me inside. I was only nine years old then, but something like this I'll never forget. My heart was broken.

This woman who put me in this orphanage was my mother's best girlfriend. They worked together at the same film lab. She had promised my mother to always take care of me. Her name was Grace Goddard. She was my aunt Grace. I learned sometime later that the day Aunt Grace took me to the orphanage she cried all morning. She did make a promise to me that as soon as she was able to she would take me out of that place. Aunt Grace came to visit me often, but when a little girl feels lonely and that nobody cares or wants her, it's just something that she can never forget as long as she lives. The promises she made to me to someday take me out of that place seemed then like only promises. I really didn't believe her.

As nice as they tried to be to me at the orphanage, it never made up for the hurt that had been done by Aunt Grace. I wanted more than anything in the world to be loved. Love to me then and now means being wanted. The world around me just crumbled. It seemed nobody wanted me, not even my mother's best friend. I was nine when I entered the orphanage and eleven when Aunt Grace finally took me out.

You know, it certainly is strange the way things work out. If Aunt Grace had not remarried, what road in life would I have taken instead? There might not have been the life in an orphanage where I was mostly miserable, living like an inmate in an institution where everyone told you, do this, do that, or you will lose your privileges of being paid to wash and dry dishes after meals, or playing with the others, or, most of all, seeing a movie.

So, instead of hating Aunt Grace for the rest of my life, I began to realize that what she did to me then hurt her so much, she felt guilty every time she would see me. Of course, I forgave her.

[When she took me out of the orphanage,] Aunt Grace did not bring me back to live with her. She took me to Van Nuys, a very poor neighborhood on the outskirts of Los Angeles. I was to live there with her aunt [Edith Ana Atchison Lower], a sixty-two-year-old spinster. Her home was a rundown bungalow, and the people in the neighborhood were mostly poor and on relief.

But I'll never forget my living there with Miss Ana Lower. She became my aunt Ana. This woman became the greatest influence in my life.

The love I have today for the simple and beautiful things in life are because of her teachings, bless her. She was one of the few persons that I really loved with such a deep love that I could only have for someone so good, so kind, and so full of love for me.

One of the many reasons I loved her so much was her philosophy, her understanding of what really mattered in life. You know, like the time when I was going to Emerson Junior High and one of the girls in my class made fun of a dress I was wearing. I don't know why kids do things like that. It really hurts so. Well, I ran home crying as though my heart would break.

My loving aunt Ana was so comforting. She just held me in her arms and rocked me to and fro like a baby and said, "It doesn't make any difference if other children make fun of you, dear—it's what you really are that counts. Just keep being yourself, honey. That's all that really matters." She was quite a person. She didn't believe in sickness, disease, or death. She didn't believe in a person being a failure, either. She did believe the mind could achieve anything it wished to achieve.

3

"HE PUT HIS HAND UNDER MY DRESS"

You wouldn't exactly say I had a normal childhood, could you? They say you soon forget the bad things in your life. Maybe for others, but not for me. I guess I was about eight years old—I was living in this foster home that took in boarders besides me. I remember there was this old man they would cater to. He was the star boarder. Well, one day when I was upstairs on the first floor where his room was, I was putting some towels in the hall closet. His door was open; he saw me and called me, motioned for me to come into his room. I went in, and immediately he bolted the door. He asked me to sit on his lap. Frightened, I obeyed. He kissed me and started doing other things to me. He put his hand under my dress. He said it's only a game. He let me go when his game was over. He touched me in places no one had ever before. When he unlocked the door and let me out, I ran to my foster mother and, crying, told her what he had done to me. "He touched me all over," I sobbed, with tears running down my face. She looked at me, shocked at what I had told her. She slapped me across the mouth and shook me, shouting, "I don't believe you. Don't you dare say such nasty things about that nice man."

I was so hurt I began to stammer. She didn't believe me. I cried all that night in my bed. I just wanted to die. This was the first time I remember ever stammering. A shocking experience like that can cause almost anything to happen. I think it caused me to stutter for the first time. There are few women who stutter. In men this is not unusual.

One day after that, when I was in the orphanage, I started to stutter out of the clear blue. I'd say to myself, Don't do that. Don't stutter. But then I'd do it again. There were times when I would do it, I couldn't get a word out.

Once in Van Nuys High School I was elected secretary to keep minutes in my English class. I began to stutter, trying to read those minutes, I'll tell you. I just happened to be a new girl in school. You just can't imagine how painful that could be. Of course, they had no way of knowing. I didn't open my mouth much, except in English, and here I was stuttering. To this day I stutter once in a while. Hardly anyone notices. It only happens when I get excited and nervous inside. I try my darnedest not to, but sometimes I do.

GEORGE BARRIS: I could see that Marilyn was a dreamer, too. She had been taken advantage of so often that she found comfort in the make-believe parts she grew up to portray on the screen. When she completed a film she could discard the character she had played and go on to another for a while, but her real life was impossible to discard. She wanted to make her past disappear, but she knew it would always return to haunt her.

Oh, sure, there were other things that happened that were unpleasant when I lived in those foster homes. Just like my being forced to live in a closet for days. There were beatings, threats, housework, and the time one of my foster parents held my head under the kitchen faucet when I was naughty. But I do remember the good things, too. I have two good memories of my childhood. I cherish them dearly, among others, of course.

One was when I had an English couple in vaudeville who were my foster parents. Although their vaudeville days were over, they taught me several things from those days. I learned how to juggle oranges, dance the hula, and how to play gin rummy. They even worked on improving my diction. That's why even to this day I have a slight British overtone in my diction if you listen carefully. To this day, listen carefully when I speak in my films—you can detect these overtones in my speech.

[The other] time was when my mother, when she was released from the hospital, bought a four-bedroom house the following year together with this English couple. Then all seemed wonderful. She even bought me a piano at an auction that once belonged to that famous movie actor Fredric March. I learned to play the classical tunes quite well. It's one of my best-kept secrets—until now of course. Very few of my friends know I can play the piano. It came in handy when I played a duet on the piano with Tom Ewell, my costar in The Seven Year Itch.

Yes, there were happy days in my life, until tragedy struck again. One day [in 1935] my mother had another breakdown. This time she was committed to the Norwalk State Hospital for Mental Diseases, where she was in and out for several years.

It was back to another foster home for me. I was now nine. I lived with my mother's best friend, until that fateful day when she committed me as my legal guardian to the orphanage. But I've already told you about this—bad fortune leading to my good fortune when I got to live with my aunt Ana.

When I was living with Aunt Ana, since Mom was in the hospital, I would go shopping with her. We were all always looking for bargains, looking to save what little money Aunt Ana had. I remember one day we were standing on a long line where they were selling day-old stale bread. For a quarter you could buy enough of the stale bread to last a week.

I thought to myself, Are we always going to be poor, standing on stale-bread lines? Sensing my sadness, Aunt Ana would squeeze my hand, smile down at me, and say to me, Norma Jeane, when you grow up, you will be a rich, beautiful, and talented lady, a famous model and actress. Only Mom and Aunt Ana knew these were my secret dreams. But guess what? When I did grow up and became a success and could afford to eat fresh bread, I was eating those melba toast breads—and they still tasted and reminded me of stale bread.

I thought to myself,
Are we always going to be poor, standing
on stale-bread lines?

4

"I WOULD PRETEND I WAS
ALICE IN WONDERLAND"

When I was a little girl I would pretend I was Alice in Wonderland looking into a mirror, wondering what I would see. Was that really me? Who was that staring back at me? Could it be someone pretending to be me? I would dance around, make faces, just to see if that little girl in the mirror would do the same.

I suppose every kid's imagination takes over. The looking glass can be magical, like acting, in a strange way. Especially when you're pretending to be someone other than yourself. This did happen when I put on my mom's clothes, tried to fix my hair as she did and powder my face with her big powder puff, and, oh yes, her red rouge and lipstick and eye shadow. I would imagine I was sexy, like the top movie star in those days, Jean Harlow.

I'm sure I looked like a clown with all that makeup, because when I made my entrance to show myself off to my mom and her friends, they just couldn't stop laughing. I started crying. Then Mom came to my rescue. She said that cosmetics were mostly used by women when they lost their natural God-given looks. She told me nature's beauty had been given to little girls. There were no cosmetics that could match this. Mom said, "I'll let you know when it's time to give nature a hand." That was my mother as I remember her. Always there when a little girl needs her mother.

I remember seeing Judy Garland in The Wizard of Oz. I sat there in a trance until my worried mother came to take me home. I asked her if there was another world out there or if it was just my imagination. Could dreams really come true? I wondered, Are the movies a make-believe land, just an illusion? Those huge images up there on the big screen in the dark theater a happy place? And looking into a mirror, Who is that looking back at me? Is it really me?

You know, children when they become adults are still at heart children. Sometimes I watch adult men. They act like little boys who have never grown up. I suppose it depends on the mood you are in. Our emotions play an important part in our lives. We cannot hide from them. My mother, bless her, used to say, "Norma Jeane, make the most of it, because that's all you've got."

GEORGE BARRIS: A quality often remarked in Marilyn was her "naturalness." She had a face that seemed ageless, and she reminded me of the barefoot contessa. She hated to wear shoes, and her golden locks were constantly falling in front of her right eye. It was easy to understand why as a nineteen-year-old model she had become so popular, so in demand for bathing suit pictures. Given her appearance on all those magazine covers then, it was only a matter of time for her to be discovered by Hollywood film studios.

Even at thirty-six, she looked and acted like a teenager. During one of our beach photography sessions, she wore a bikini that revealed almost all of the physical Marilyn.

Being poor those early years acted in some ways as a blessing in disguise. I didn't have the money to go to beauty parlors for permanents or facials, so I learned to do with what nature blessed me with, the natural look.

You know, I don't remember using makeup until I was twelve years old. That was when I was attending Emerson Junior High in Van Nuys. What got me started was that the other girls were doing it. I felt if I didn't at least use some makeup, they would snub me and I would feel out of place. Girls can do that. Believe me. They loaded their faces and hair with permanents, false eyelashes, eye shadow, mascara, rouge, powder, and loads of lipstick, with a touch of Vaseline to give their lips the moist look they were told makes them alluring. Me, I used very little lipstick. That was all.

I used to laugh to myself when I'd see these girls all made-up. They really looked awful, but I would never tell them. You know, girls that age would think I was just jealous. The boys at our school would make fun of these girls, telling them clowns at the circus looked better than they did. Me? The boys never would laugh at me. All they wanted to do was touch me all over. But my mom told me to tell them, Just keep your hands to yourself!

Even then, at twelve, when I wore a tight skirt and sweater, the boy's eyes would pop and they would whistle at me and just stare. It's true I started to blossom out in all directions at that tender age, in the front and the rear, too. In the front my boobs were

Well after she had become adept at the artifice of makeup, she was willing to show her public the real Marilyn Monroe, the real Norma Jeane. She would hide nothing in our photos. No magic, no makeup or retouching of our finished photographs.

At an interval in the shoot, a fan came up and asked me a question. He had noted the scar on Marilyn's stomach (from her gall bladder surgery), the prominent freckles on her arms and body, including her legs, and he even mentioned the traces of babylike fuzz on her face. Why didn't these "flaws" show up in photographs of the star? When I told this to Marilyn, she laughed and said, "Well, I guess that only proves I'm human."

_____

sprouting and in the rear my little tush became more firm and round. Like the boys would say, it looked like I was carrying two melons up front and two more in the rear. The boys would get excited. They'd say that Norma Jeane shakes like Jell-O, up and down and even sideways. I'd let some of the nice boys walk me home, but it was always, "Hands off, guys." If I liked a certain boy after he walked me home, when there was no one around I'd let him hug me and give me a peck on the cheek, but no funny stuff, as we called it in those days.

The boys knew better than to get fresh with me. The most they could expect was a good-night kiss on the cheek, and, as I told you before, if I really liked a boy he could

give me a hug around the waist friendly-like. I'd wrestle with the boys on the beach in a friendly way. Every boy wanted to wrestle with me.

I always looked older than my age, I guess it was my growing-up time. You know, some kids develop sooner than others. Why, when I was only ten, I shot up to my full height of five feet, five inches, except I was skinny and looked boyish. But when I was twelve, I all of a sudden became a sweater girl and caused a sensation where the boys were concerned.

At thirteen everyone said I looked eighteen, and the boys in their twenties were trying to date me. I may still have been a baby on the inside, but on the outside I had

the body of a woman. The boys would always whistle and flirt as if I was the only girl on the block. I started dating when I was thirteen. All the other girls became jealous of me. I guess they were afraid of losing their boyfriends.

Just three weeks after my sixteenth birthday, I was married to the boy next door, Jim Dougherty. In those days I would be considered a child bride. I guess even by today's standards I'd be considered one, too.

Guess who designed my wedding gown? Aunt Ana. I was so proud; I was listed as her niece on my marriage certificate. You know, at my first wedding I had six mothers claiming me and all weeping when I marched down the aisle. I guess they all considered me their daughter even though they were my foster mothers only—at one time or another in my young life.

I didn't know anything about marriage, especially the sex part of it, and I was scared to death of what a husband would do to me—but I'll tell you more about this later on.

*I may still have been a baby on the inside,
but on the outside I had the body of a woman.*

5

"I THOUGHT I WAS
TOO COLD, FRIGID"

et me tell you more about how my marriage to Jim Dougherty developed. When I was still fifteen Aunt Grace decided to get me off her hands, even though she was my legal guardian. The best way she thought was for me to get married. I remember her telling me, "Norma Jeane, you really are now quite a mature woman," and that it was time for me to think about marriage.

Wow. This really frightened me. I had never thought about marriage. You know, going with boys was fun and all that, but marriage, no. I was only fifteen. Maybe I looked like a woman, but I was still a kid. I protested to Aunt Grace. "But I'm too young," I pleaded. Her answer: "Only in years, only in years. You're really quite a mature woman, even though you are only fifteen." It was all my aunt Grace's doing; she instigated my marriage to Jim Dougherty. Jim was older—around twenty-one, going on twenty-two.

We dated for several months to get to know each other better. I never had an engagement. And just three weeks after my June first birthday was when we had our double-ring ceremony. Marriage to Jim brought me escape at the time. It was that or my being sent off again to another foster home. Once more it was the case of not being wanted. It wasn't fair to push me into marriage. What did I know about sex? When I told Aunt Grace I was frightened of what a husband might do to me, she seemed quite surprised at my innocence.

What shocked me the most then was finding out before marriage that I was an illegitimate child! Then finding out for the first time the true facts of life. My aunt Ana bought me a book that contained the facts and hints a bride-to-be should know. I had told my aunt Grace I didn't feel confident that I could be a good wife. I thought I was too cold, frigid.

After our marriage, Jim said I was a most responsive bride, perfect in every respect— except in the cooking department. I was a warm, loving wife. If only I could cook.

GEORGE BARRIS: When Marilyn turned sixteen, she was practically forced to get married. Otherwise she probably would have had to live in another foster home. Jim Dougherty seemed a nice enough sort of young man. Yes, she said, he was a nice, caring person— but marriage at age sixteen for the rest of her life? Didn't loving your husband count? What about the intimate part of marriage?

Sex and marriage no doubt scared the life out of Norma Jeane. She was still a virgin. Maybe she did let the boys kiss her, maybe she even petted a little—but that was all. It didn't mean she was ready to be a bride. She and Jim did as best they could.

Marilyn and Jim spent many of the early days of their marriage at Santa Monica's "Muscle Beach," which was famous for its

Jim never wanted me to become a model or actress. In fact, he never encouraged me in any way. He would discourage me by telling me that there were plenty of beautiful girls that could sing and dance and act. Hollywood was full of them. They're all looking for work. What, he would say to me, what makes you think you're any better than them? I don't think he really knew how I felt.

It was 1944, during World War Two, that Jim enlisted in the U.S. Merchant Marine. After his boot training he was stationed at Catalina Island, not far from where we had been living in Los Angeles. He was a physical training instructor there, and the best part was I was able to join him. It was a world of men, all sailors with their wives and families. I didn't mind it being a world of men as long as I was a woman in it. You never saw so many sailors, so many men.

Besides the sailors there, [there were some] marines, Seabees, coast guardsmen—but not too many girls. I was always true to my husband, but he seemed jealous and annoyed when the men would whistle at me. He would lecture me about the type of clothes I was wearing. Actually, I wore the same clothes the other girls wore, you know, tight sweaters, shorts, and what Jim would call bathing suits. I just couldn't understand his acting that way.

population of handsome men who gathered there to show off their feats of strength. The young couple would relax and watch the muscle men perform. When Jim was not around, many of those young men would flirt with Marilyn and ask her for dates. All she had to do to discourage them was to smile and flash her wedding band, saying "Sorry." She was faithful in those days.

Photographing Marilyn, I sometimes wondered how she could possibly be faithful to one man. As she would say, "I wish there were more of me to make all those men out there happy." I often thought she had been blessed with too much in this world; men desired her and women were envious of her beauty. I hoped her life would bring her happiness someday.

When Jim was shipped to Shanghai, I went back to Van Nuys to live with his family. I got a job at the Radio Plane plant in Burbank [a defense plant]. They started me there as a parachute inspector, and later I was promoted to the "dope room," where I would spray this liquid dope, which is made by mixing banana oil and glue, on the planes' fuselages. These were miniature planes used for target practice. The dope was sprayed on the fuselage to give it strength. I worked in overalls and kept my head covered most of the time so that the dope wouldn't get into my hair, since it was messy and difficult to wash out.

Well, one day an army photographer came to our plant. He was from the army's pictorial center in Hollywood. His assignment was to take pictures for the army newspapers and magazines of people working in defense plants, showing them doing their share in the war effort. He called them morale-booster photos. I was later told most of these photos were of pretty girls at work.

So when this army photographer, David Conover, passed by where I was working, he says, "You are a real morale booster. I'm going to take your picture for the boys in the army to keep their morale high." I didn't know what he was talking about at that time, but he later explained it to me. First he took pictures of me in my overalls, but when he discovered I had a sweater in my locker, he asked if I would mind wearing it for more pictures. He said, "I want to show the boys what you really look like."

Those pictures he took of me were the first that ever appeared in a publication. They appeared in hundreds of army camp newspapers, including the army's famous Yank magazine and Stars and Stripes.

When David Conover phoned me a few weeks later, he said he had shown my pictures to a commercial photographer friend in Los Angeles and if I was interested in modeling he would like to see me. I soon called the photographer, Potter Hueth, and made an appointment to see him. At his studio he explained to me that he couldn't pay me for modeling then, but if I wanted to speculate with him he would take pictures of me

and when he sold them to the magazines he would pay me. *The fee, he said, was usually five to ten dollars an hour, which was a lot of money in those days.*

What did I have to lose? So I agreed, providing I could pose at night so as not to lose time from my job. That was okay with him. I worked at his studio several nights. He told me I had that natural look. I told him I always tried to be natural. Secretly I'd always wanted to be a photographer's model. Maybe this would be the beginning for me.

6

"IT'S JUST TOO MUCH SEX THAT YOU HAVE"

My career as a model started when Potter Hueth showed the pictures he took of me to Miss [Emmeline] Snively, who then ran the largest model agency in Los Angeles. I was quite excited when she agreed to see me. An appointment was made, and I couldn't sleep the night before. If she didn't like me, that would be the end of my modeling career—before it started.

Calling in sick, I took the day off to go see Miss Snively. I was then nineteen, my marriage was strained, and I was thinking of a divorce. When I wrote to my husband, I explained I did not love him anymore, that I had a chance for a career as a model, and that I wanted freedom to pursue my career. I wanted a divorce.

Jim was still in Shanghai. He wrote asking if I would wait until he returned from overseas to see if we could patch things up and make a go of our marriage. But I knew our marriage was over. A career was more important to me. I wanted to become an actress more than ever. Perhaps through modeling I would get the break I needed.

At the appointed hour—eleven A.M.—I entered Miss Snively's office. I was nervous and hoped it didn't show. During the interview she told me I had the makings of a model but that I would have to attend the modeling school she also operated. This, she told me, was necessary so that I could be properly groomed. The school's tuition would be one hundred dollars. I told her, "Well, that lets me out." I did not have the money. She said not to worry, that I could pay her out of the modeling jobs she would get for me.

I can still remember the first modeling job I ever had. I was a hostess at an aluminum exhibit at the Los Angeles Home Show in the Pan Pacific Auditorium. I received ten dollars a day for ten days, and all of it went to paying for my modeling lessons.

My second modeling job did not turn out so well. In fact, it was quite bad. With a group of models I went on a photo assignment to model sport clothes for a famous

GEORGE BARRIS: As a nineteen-year-old, Marilyn had spent many happy days modeling at Santa Monica beach on assignments from Miss Snively's modeling agency. She had been the agency's top "cheesecake" model; magazine and newspaper editors were constantly assigning photographers to take pictures of the sexy Norma Jeane. Later on, when I had the opportunity to photograph Marilyn in the same location, I know she was reminded of her youthful days on the sunny beach, and she told me that the pictures I took of her there were her favorites of them all.

Her success as a model had enabled Norma Jeane to leave her aunt Ana then and to move into her own small apartment. Her mother, Gladys, had been released from a hospital stay and came to live with her

American catalogue. The location was Malibu beach. After two days they sent me home. They would not tell me why. I was very upset—here I was the only model in the group fired.

Later I found out the reason I was fired. They said no one would ever look at the clothes in their catalogue. Miss Snively later told me it's just you have more than the usual amount of sex appeal. It's just too much sex that you have to be a fashion model.

I believed in myself so much that I would make it as a model I quit my job at the defense plant. I was determined I would be able to succeed as a model. I never missed my modeling school classes. I always did the best I could. I wouldn't settle for second best. I had so much confidence in myself I just knew I could make it. I would take home photographs of myself to study how I looked and if I could improve myself posing in front of a mirror for hours.

The next day I would see the photographer who took those pictures and ask, What did I do wrong in this photo? or Why didn't this photo come out better? When they told me, I would never make that mistake again. I believed in myself. I just had to make it. I was determined to make it. Nothing was going to get in my way.

Then they started to put me in bathing suits, and all of a sudden I became popular.

daughter there. They slept in the same bed. Acting as her daughter's secretary, Gladys took phone messages and made appointments for her. For a while all was well.

Gladys couldn't do enough for her daughter. She ran errands, went shopping, and even traveled by streetcar to the Ambassador Hotel, where Miss Snively's modeling agency was located, to thank her personally for being so helpful to Norma Jeane's career.

All this came to my mind as Marilyn reviewed those Santa Monica beach photos, recalling her modeling days as a determined young girl who yearned to become a movie star. I don't think anyone was ever more determined, and I never encountered a model who worked as hard as she did.

Photographers liked working with me. They said I knew how to take direction. I began having lots of location assignments. It was like I had been discovered. I was in great demand for bathing suit pictures. In those days I was a brunette. Miss Snively kept insisting I become a blonde. But I refused, I didn't want to bleach my hair. But she kept telling me, "Norma Jeane, if you expect to go places, you've got to be a blonde."

I refused because I felt I wouldn't feel natural. It would not be me. Miss Snively carefully explained to me that photographers with their lighting techniques can photograph a blonde differently, light or dark, and those in-between-shades, by controlling their lighting. "You'll become more successful than you are now, believe me," she said. "But you've got to become a blonde." I finally agreed to it when the photographer Raphael Wolff agreed to pay for the bleaching. I had long hair in those days, and they cut it short and then styled it in an upsweep. When I saw myself in the mirror, it just wasn't the real me. They had converted me to a golden blonde. At first I couldn't get used to myself.

But then I saw it worked. Miss Snively sure knew what she was telling me. I began to get more modeling assignments in photography for glamour poses, and especially cheesecake pictures. And the talk came back to what photographers were saying about me: That Norma Jeane—she's built like a sex machine. She could turn it on and off.

I couldn't believe what they were saying about me. The word was around: "Don't let anyone tell you it's in her hips or her bosom; you know where it is, it's in her mind." I couldn't believe what was happening to me. I began to appear in all of the magazines of the day, especially the men's.

But let me fill you in with the details. You know, when Howard Hughes saw my picture on a magazine cover, the mere fact that word got out to the Fox studio talent agent Ben Lyon that [Hughes was interested in me] was enough for Fox to take notice and then want to give me that screen test in color. The interesting thing was [Lyon] didn't even ask me if I had any acting experience. He did not ask me to read any scripts. Nothing. Mr. Lyon himself in the 1920s and 30s was a big movie star—he costarred with Jean Harlow in the film Hell's Angels—but now he was a talent scout for the studio.

Darryl Zanuck was head of the studio, and he had to approve all color film tests, but he was out of town. We would have to wait for his return. So the secret movie screen test was made of me while Mr. Zanuck was away.

7

"NOW I'M MARILYN MONROE"

*L*et me tell you more about my first screen test at Fox. It was a silent test. There was no dialogue. Mr. Leon Shamroy was the motion picture cameraman who they said was the best in the business. He would photograph my screen test. [At the time] there was a film in production called Mother Wore Tights, with Betty Grable.

Secretly one morning around five thirty, Mr. Shamroy and myself sneaked on the set. I made up in a portable dressing room that Mr. Lyon sneaked out of wardrobe. [The dress] was lovely, a sequined evening gown for me to wear for my big scene. Mr. Shamroy lighted the set himself and loaded his motion picture camera and served as his own camera operator.

We rehearsed my first big scene and then I began the scene and prayed silently that this was my start, the beginning of becoming a motion picture actress. This is what my big scene consisted of: I walked across the set; I had to light a cigarette, inhale, then blow the smoke out, get up, then go upstage, cross, look out a window, sit down, come downstage, and then exit the set. Those bright lights were blinding me, and for some strange reason—instead of being nervous and scared as I thought I'd be—I just did the best I could.

I tried very hard, I did my best, because I knew Mr. Lyon and Mr. Shamroy were taking an awful chance if the test didn't work out well. They'd be in a lot of trouble, maybe even fired. Darryl Zanuck I was told was a tyrant, a real SOB. I just couldn't let them down; most of all I couldn't let myself down. This is what I wanted more than anything else. This is what I'd been waiting for—I just had to make it.

Both men privately screened my test without my being invited. I guess if it was a flop they didn't want me to see it. But Mr. Shamroy did confess to me later on that watching my screen test he got a cold chill. The girl up there on that screen had something he had not seen since the days of silent pictures. This girl had sex on a piece of film like Jean Harlow had. Every frame of that film radiated. And all this without a sound track. Up there was a girl, the first he had seen that he said looked like one of those lush silent-days screen stars. He explained that I had shown I could sell emotions, sex in pictures. He claimed that was stirring the audience. Movies are pictures that create

GEORGE BARRIS: Marilyn once told me that only a few men had helped her in the early days of her career. She knew that she had the physical beauty, personality, desire, and talent she needed. But in Hollywood, where every girl wanted to be in films, she soon discovered that knowing the "right people" in the industry could open doors for her. One of the men who helped the most early on was Ben Lyon.

A Twentieth Century-Fox talent scout, Lyon, along with Leon Shamroy, the stu-

emotions, not just people up there opening and closing their mouths. "And, baby," he said, "you certainly have got it!"

Ben Lyon agreed, and was so excited that he sneaked my test into the daily film rushes that Mr. Zanuck would be viewing. "Who is that girl?" and "Who authorized that screen test?" Zanuck shouted. Quite nervous, Ben Lyon admitted he had made the test on his own. There was tension in the air. Zanuck, taking a deep puff on his cigar and blowing out the smoke, was silent for a while. Lyon, holding his breath, wondered if he and Shamroy would get the ax. "That's a damn fine test. Who is the girl? I hope you signed her," shouted Zanuck. The gamble these men took on me paid off.

"Now Norma Jeane," Mr. Lyon said, "take this contract home and have your legal guardian sign it." When I got home and showed the contract to my aunt Grace, who was my legal guardian, I also told her my new name as an actress would be Marilyn, as suggested by Mr. Lyon. Before I could tell her what my last name would be, Aunt Grace said, "Sounds fine for a first name. Why not use your mother's maiden name Monroe for your last name?" With this, I hesitated, then replied, "Well, I don't

"And, baby," he said, "you certainly have got it!"

dio's great cinematographer, shot the test without the authorization of the all-powerful Darryl Zanuck. On the set of a Betty Grable movie at five in the morning, Marilyn, wearing a gown borrowed from wardrobe, had her secret screen test.

Zanuck's highly favorable response when he viewed the test ensured that a starlet was born. And Norma Jeane Mortenson was no more. She became Marilyn Monroe. She was just twenty years old.

know." But Aunt Grace insisted it would make [my] mother so proud if [I] did. Then I laughed and shouted to Aunt Grace, "I thought so, too. Now I'm Marilyn Monroe." We all started to laugh as Aunt Grace gave me a big hug. She said, "That's my girl." From that day on, I had to get used to my new name—I'd better remember who I was. Most important, I'd better know how to spell my name, too. What if someday someone asked me for my autograph and I signed it Jeane—or even if I didn't know how to spell Marilyn Monroe!

With a new name and a studio contract, my new life had begun. I was on my way to being a film actress. What I'd been dreaming for now had happened. Photography had shown I was what they were looking for up there on the silver screen. Now I had to prove I could act. For voice parts, I was told I would be given lessons at the studio's school that they had for what they called their "starlets," of which I was now one.

Later that year, Jim [Dougherty] finally gave in and signed our divorce papers. I was granted a divorce in Reno, Nevada, just six weeks before I had signed my movie contract with one of the largest motion picture studios, Twentieth Century–Fox. And I was now twenty years old.

Life is certainly strange. It seems like only yesterday. It's amazing how much a person's mind has the capacity for recalling. In my mind I was on my way to stardom, but to the studio I was just another starlet who, if she was lucky enough, would get a small walk-on or speak a word or two that you wouldn't even notice if you're not a careful observer during a movie. In other words, I had been told it is unusual for a starlet to become a star. This I would find out for myself the hard way.

For the first six months I worked very hard, attending classes in acting, pantomime, singing, voice, and dancing. I could never afford all this on my own. I could thank my lucky stars it was all free.

8

FIRST MOVIE BREAK: *SCUDDA-HOO!*

I had done everything the studio people asked me to do, and yet I hadn't appeared in one motion picture. Six months had gone by. According to my seven-year contract, the studio could take advantage of renewing my contract for another six months or they could just drop me. That's what the small print in my contract stated. If they picked up my contract, which is called the option, I would also get a raise. I was so nervous I couldn't sleep nights. I even prayed real hard.

My prayers were answered. My contract was picked up; I got my raise. My salary was doubled. It would now be one hundred fifty dollars per week. From seventy-five dollars a week. Wow! I really went to town. I was so excited, I went out and bought five hundred dollars' worth of clothes. Up to that time I had been making ends meet with what I had. (I was only twenty-one).

But the real excitement came when I got my first movie role. The film was Scudda-Hoo! Scudda-Hay! June Haver played the lead, and, if you watched the movie real close during the dancing, you would see a sixty-second close-up of my back during one of those dancing numbers. I guess the studio didn't think enough of my back scene, and the next time my contract option came up they let me go. It was August 1947. What a blow to my ego. What a blow to my career.

I was back where I had started. I moved back into the Studio Club to my one furnished room where I had lived before. The Studio Club was a low-cost club for struggling models and aspiring actresses. The apartment I had before I could no longer afford. I went back to modeling, but when you're out of sight, it's true, you're also out of mind, that is, the photographer's mind. After all, I had been under contract to Twentieth Century–Fox studios for a year, and as far as the photographers knew, I was out of circulation, not available.

Now that I had to pay for my acting lessons, I often went without eating. That was my ambition in life—to be an actress, so I just had to keep improving myself to prove to myself and others that I was serious.

GEORGE BARRIS: Another of Marilyn's powerful mentors (and many maintain he was much more than that) was Joe Schenck, the cofounder of Fox studios. He became her close friend and benefactor, and when Zanuck refused to renew her six-month option contract despite Schenck's pleas, Schenck persuaded his friend Harry Cohn, head of Columbia Pictures, to sign Marilyn. Although word had it that Marilyn was the mistress of the long-married but frequently faithless Schenck, she always denied it.

Her vocal coach at Columbia was Freddy Karger, who was given the assignment to help Marilyn develop her singing voice for *Ladies of the Chorus*. The two became friends, then lovers. At one time she pleaded with him to marry her, but he refused, telling her she would not be a suitable mother for his daughter from a previ-

Of course, there are other ways a girl could survive until another studio came along. A starlet could take on a lover, usually a well-heeled married man who could pay her bills, or she could become the mistress to an old man and through his connections help advance her career. Believe me, there were and still are many starstruck girls that do get by that way. But for myself, respect is one of life's greatest treasures. I mean, what does it all add up to if you don't have that? If there [is] only one thing in my life I [am] proud of, it's that I've never been a kept woman.

And believe me, it wasn't because there weren't opportunities to become one. I think I had as many problems as the next starlet keeping the Hollywood wolves from my door. These wolves just could not understand me. They would tell me, "But Marilyn, you're not playing the game the way you should. Be smart. You'll never get anywhere in this business acting the way you do." My answer to them would be, "The only acting I'll do is for the motion picture camera." I was determined, no one was going to use me or my body—even if he could help my career. I've never gone out with a man I didn't want to. No one, not even the studio, could force me to date someone.

The one thing I hate more than anything else is being used. I've always worked hard for the sake of someday becoming a talented actress. I knew I would make it

ous marriage because she was too wrapped up in her career. Heartbroken, she remained friends with Freddy, and with his family. The couple continued to date on and off.

Yet another powerful man in Marilyn's life was Johnny Hyde, vice president of the influential William Morris Agency. Johnny had a talent for creating superstars, such as Rita Hayworth. He had seen Marilyn's screen test and, like Zanuck, been hugely impressed; he had to meet her. Many other starlets were trying to make it, but from that mass of flesh Johnny Hyde knew a winner: Marilyn had that "something" that stars are made of. He knew she was destined for stardom; Johnny wanted to help her get there.

Johnny got her most of her bit parts in her early days as a starlet. He explained that it wasn't the size of a film part, but the exposure itself that got the attention of pro-

someday if I only kept at it and worked hard without lowering my principles and pride in myself.

For the next six months I managed to get by on unemployment insurance benefits. When that ran out I would give my friends I.O.U. notes when they loaned me money to get by on. There were not too many modeling jobs then. The few I did have helped. There was one thing—I never stopped taking drama lessons even when I did go hungry at times. Anyway, doing so was good for my figure, I told myself. Besides, what would make me an actress, acting lessons or hamburgers? No one had to tell me what to do. My mind was made up as long as I could remember—that's what I wanted most. This being an actress may have started out as a dream, but I was determined that one day it would all come true.

Then, six months later on the strength of the screen test I had made at Fox, Columbia Pictures hired me at the usual starlet salary being paid then—one hundred twenty-five dollars a week. Boy, was I in heaven. It was like my going to school and being paid for it. They had me study with the studio's drama coach, Natasha Lytess. When I first read for her, she said my voice sounded like a squeak and the first thing she would have to teach me was diction. I said I'd do anything, whatever she thought would make me an actress.

Most important before anything else, if you want to be an actress, you must always remember your lines. Never, never, she said, go on a set without knowing your lines,

ducers, directors, and studio heads. Enough exposure and they'd all want to know who you were.

And Johnny again proved to be right. He took Marilyn everywhere, to make sure she'd be seen by the right people. They went to premieres, Hollywood parties, and all the right clubs. She was only twenty-two, and Hollywood knew her name.

know them backwards and forwards so if [you] had to throw away the words [you] could speak the soul of the lines. She was the first person of authority I met who believed I could make a fine actress if I worked hard at it, and most important I promised I would—since that's what I wanted most. She promised me she would help me.

This, my second picture, was what is called a quickie film. It was filmed in only eleven days. The name of the film was Ladies of the Chorus. My role in this film was that of a strip-teaser in a burlesque show. I got to sing and dance, but even with special coaching from Fred Karger, who was musical director, the film did not create any excitement. But my first notice in the Motion Picture Herald [a trade paper] appeared on October 23, 1948. The paper's reviewer wrote: "One of the brightest spots is Miss Monroe's singing. She is pretty, and with her pleasing voice and style shows promise."

Even with this "rave," the studio was not overly impressed. When my contract came up for renewal that September they dropped me. I was shocked.

*Besides, what would make
me an actress,
acting lessons or hamburgers?*

9

"NICE GIRLS DID NOT POSE IN THE NUDE"

It was back in 1948, when Columbia Pictures did not pick up my contract option, that it was back to modeling. When jobs were few and far between, that's when I posed for what became the world-famous nude calendar picture. I was really broke. Oh, there were some modeling jobs—but not enough to pay the bills—and there was a payment on my car or I would lose it. And without a car it's almost impossible to get around in Los Angeles.

There was this photographer, Tom Kelley. I had worked for him before. He kept asking me if I would pose for him in the nude as a calendar girl. I kept telling him no thanks. I'll work the usual five-dollar and ten-dollar model fees—not that there was anything wrong posing nude for a calendar.

It just was not something I could do. But Kelley always would say, "If you ever change your mind, just call me anytime."

So you see, it was when I really had no work and no money. Out of desperation I called Tom Kelley and asked him, was he still willing to pay me fifty dollars for that calendar shoot posing in the nude? When he told me he still would pay me that price, I said, "I need that fifty dollars. You must promise never to tell anyone about my posing for you in the nude. I want you to promise me that you will take the pictures so that I wouldn't be recognizable in them." Mr. Kelley promised me that no one would ever know except him and his wife, who acted as his assistant. I was desperate. I was nearly broke. What else could I do?

I arrived at his studio and, as agreed, only he and his wife were there. Mr. Kelley draped the background in red velvet. Me, I was completely nude. But Tom Kelley's wife, Natalie, being there helped calm my nervousness. (A few years ago when the photographer André de Dienes wanted me to pose in the nude I told him I would never, no never. I told him nice girls did not pose in the nude.)

But now I was desperate. Fifty dollars in those days in 1948 was a lot of money. I

GEORGE BARRIS: Photographers, both of stills and movies, were of critical importance in establishing Marilyn's career from the very beginning. Many of the best known during her heyday did some of their finest work with Marilyn as their subject. It has been often said that she loved the camera and that the camera loved her right back.

One photographer who played a significant role in her professional and personal life was André de Dienes, one of the leading glamour lensmen of his day. His photos of Norma Jeane made the covers of the top magazines and brought national recognition to the then unknown young beauty. André once told me he was in love with Norma Jeane and that she had at one time promised to marry him. She changed her mind—but they remained close friends.

My late friend Milton H. Greene, another well-known photographer of the time, was on one occasion on assignment in

posed for Mr. Kelley two hours and signed the model release, "Mona Monroe." I don't know why, except I may have wanted to protect myself. I was nervous, embarrassed, even ashamed of what I had done, and I did not want my name to appear on that model release.

Kelley, I was later told, sold the nude photo of me to the Western Lithograph Company for nine hundred dollars, and the calendar made millions, especially three years later, when I was back at Fox studios. The calendar, called "Golden Dreams," earned millions for that company when it became known that I was that nude calendar girl. Me? All I was ever paid for that nude calendar photograph was the fifty dollars Tom paid me as the original modeling fee.

It was this famous nude photo of me Hugh Hefner bought for just five hundred dollars, plus another photo of me fully dressed, to launch his first issue of Playboy, for the cover and nude girl inside.

In the picture used on that first-issue cover of that man's magazine I was seated on top of a huge elephant at a circus benefit in New York's Madison Square Garden. The magazine, I was told, thanks to my photos, [was] an instant sellout all across the

Hollywood to photograph Marilyn for *Look* magazine. She liked him—but even more she liked his ideas. They became friends, too, and Milton persuaded Marilyn to go into business with him. She could be more than an actress. "Let's be partners and make our own pictures," he insisted, until she agreed. The only film their company, Marilyn Monroe Productions, made was *The Prince and the Showgirl*, which costarred and was directed by Laurence Olivier.

There were many others—and one day, when I was thinking about these colleagues, Marilyn came up to me and said, "A penny for your thoughts."

I said, "Oh, just daydreaming—about all the famous photographers in your life."

"I hope you've included yourself," she replied.

It was impossible to buy Marilyn's affection, and I was both flattered and pleased by what she had said.

country, an instant success. I never even received a thank-you from all those who made millions off a nude Marilyn photograph. I even had to buy a copy of the magazine to see myself in it. A copy of the nude calendar was bought and given to me by a friend. Years later I gave it to my then husband, Joe DiMaggio.

I admitted it was me who posed for that nude calendar even when the Fox executives became nervous and believed this would cause the ruination of any films I would appear in and also the end of my movie career.

Of course they were wrong. The fans, my public, cheered when I admitted it was me, and that calendar and that Playboy first-issue publicity helped my career. Stories appeared in all the newspapers. The calendar picture of me was finally considered a work

of art. At first the U.S. Post Office refused [to permit] the calendar to be sent by mail. It was classified as pornographic, and even some states put a ban on it being sold there.

My career was now in gear. My third film came about when an actress I met while having lunch at the Schwab's famous Sunset Boulevard drugstore mentioned they were filming a Marx Brothers film at the R.K.O. studios and were looking for a blonde. Not being a blonde, she told me, "Why don't you try for it? What have you got to lose?" She gave me the producer's phone number. I phoned Lester Cowan, told him I was a blonde. His reply was, "But are you a sexy blonde?" I told him I had had no complaints yet. Well, then he told me to come over immediately.

When I got to the studio, I had to wait hours. The Marx Brothers were at lunch.

When they got back, they told me I wouldn't have any lines to speak. All the talking I would have to do was with my body. Actually [the role] was just a walk-on, but the walking would be most important. Groucho asked me if I could walk in a way to make smoke come out of his head. I told him I could. I walked across the room, and when I turned around there was smoke coming out of Groucho's head!

I wasn't supposed to have any speaking lines in this picture, but Groucho improvised some lines for me. My part consisted of walking into his office. In the movie he plays a detective. When he asks what can he do for me, I answer, "Men keep following me all the time." Then I walk out of his office. That's all. This scene couldn't have lasted more than sixty seconds on the screen.

My screen appearances to date had been limited to a big sixty seconds. [This particular] minute on the screen worked wonders for me. Lester Cowan, the producer, actually had his press agents making me the star of the film. Me with that one little scene. But let me tell you more about what happened to me later on. It could only happen in Hollywood.

*I never even received a thank-you
from all those who made millions off a
nude Marilyn photograph.*

10

"I'M FINALLY OUT OF SIXTY-SECOND SCENES"

What happened to me because of [that] sixty seconds in the Marx Brothers film, Love Happy, could only happen in Hollywood. Imagine, Lester Cowan, the producer, made me a star of that film even though I had only one scene and one line. I was sent to some of the larger cities in the country on a personal appearance tour for five weeks.

I felt guilty when I appeared on the stage of those movie houses billed as the star. It really was embarrassing. I had never traveled like this. For the first time I lived the life of a big Hollywood movie star, which I certainly was not. In all these cities I had press interviews, my picture in the newspapers. I appeared on television, on the radio, and, while in New York my photographer friend André de Dienes, who was working there then, took me to Jones Beach. He took pictures of me. It was fun and relaxing from the mad pace of interviews for the movie.

After those hectic five weeks, it was like Cinderella after the ball. I was back in Hollywood, wondering where or when my next film role would be offered to me. Nothing happened for some time.

Then that old screen test came to my rescue once more. Someone accidentally sent my color screen test over to Metro-Goldwyn-Mayer studios, along with others they had requested. I was excited.

They didn't have any part for me in their films then, but one of their casting agents, Lucille Ryman, told me what I'd always wanted to hear. Miss Ryman said I had talent as an actress. Up to then no one had told me this. She told me to count on her as a friend. Can you imagine! This was music to my ears.

GEORGE BARRIS: In 1948, Marilyn auditioned in front of producer Arthur Hornblow Jr. and director John Huston for a part in their film *Asphalt Jungle*. She tried out for the role of Angela Phinlay, mistress to a crooked lawyer. At first she did not win the part, but then boyfriend Johnny Hyde was influential in getting her a second, successful chance. Her portrayal brought her good though brief critical notice.

It was interesting to observe Marilyn's body language when she studied a script. A wide variety of facial and vocal techniques were at her beck and call. Here are some characteristic techniques she might employ.

Marilyn would start out lying on her back quite calmly, which appeared to be a most relaxing way for her to study her script. She would hold the script high over her head, then against her body. She would raise one foot as high as she could, relaxing the other with her knee bent. She would turn her head from side to side, sometimes closing her eyes as if in a deep sleep.

She might kneel on all fours, like a cat ready to pounce, looking down at her script as if she were ready to attack. She would assume this position when she was reading a dramatic part, rocking herself back and forth.

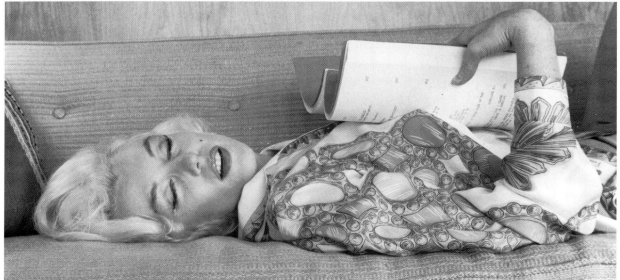

She proved a wonderful person. She let me live with her so that I wouldn't have to worry about modeling or making the casting rounds. Now, because of her, I was able to study my dramatics, singing, and dancing without any worries. I felt I had a guardian angel looking after me. I was sure it was my aunt Ana, may God bless her.

Nothing much happened for a while, until Miss Ryman told me she had just finished reading a script that her studio was making into a movie. It was called Asphalt Jungle. She felt there was a part in it for me that might skyrocket my career. She told a wonderful guy named Johnny Hyde, vice president of the top Hollywood talent agency, William Morris, about this, and he agreed to take me over to the studio to meet the producer, Arthur Hornblow, and the director, John Huston.

Mr. Huston said I looked right for the part and gave me the script to study. No, I didn't have the part yet. He suggested I come back when I thought I was ready to audition the scene of the girl in the story, Angela. The day I returned to Mr. Huston's

From a position on the couch with the script on the floor, laughing and giggling, she might become hysterical if the scene depicted a humorous or fantastic event.

Marilyn would often try to dig deep down into her subconscious for some past event that would relate to the character she had to portray. This would help her to convey the emotional content needed for that character and scene. As she took on thephysical aspect of the character she was portraying, her voice would even change. One moment she would yell, then laugh, then cry, even sing.

In 1949, Marilyn landed the small part of Miss Caswell in *All About Eve,* one of Hollywood's finest films ever. Beautifully playing a girl who would do anything to get ahead, her performance won her a new contract at Twentieth Century-Fox, and a rapid succession of roles were to follow.

She was increasingly noticed in the press, whose importance to her career she recognized. "You've got to see that they put your name and picture before your fans so that they don't forget you," she once told me. She liked most reporters and photographers, but she distrusted the ones she called "mud-slingers," those who searched out embarrassing gossip and scandals.

But the few she truly trusted became her loyal friends for life. One of these was Sidney Skolsky, a New York press agent and columnist who fell in love with Hollywood and its stars and made himself a home in California, setting up his "office" in the famous Schwab's Drugstore on Sunset Boulevard. During Marilyn's early days in Hollywood, Skolsky would let her know when he heard of a part being cast that he thought would suit her. He would talk her up to the studio, and if he could convince those in charge to see her, he would phone her to let her know.

Thanks to Sidney's persuasive ways, he was able to talk R.K.O. producer Jerry Wald into considering Marilyn for the part of a sex-wild girl named Peggy in Wald's next film, *Clash by Night*. Skolsky suggested to Marilyn that she wear her sexiest dress to

meet with Wald, who was an anomaly among Hollywood power brokers—he was happily married and not looking for sexual favors in exchange for professional opportunity. When Wald eyed the gorgeous Marilyn, he said immediately, "You *are* Peggy." Marilyn cried when she got the part.

Not only did Skolsky act as Marilyn's agent; on occasion he served as her escort to various Hollywood functions, including the

1953 *Photoplay* awards, where she received the Gold Medal as outstanding new actress of the year. Joan Crawford, then in her late forties, was so upset at the ceremonies by the sight of Marilyn in a shockingly low-cut gold sheath that she exclaimed to the press, "Look, there's nothing wrong with my tits—but you will never see me flaunting them in the public's faces." (Crawford's anger might have been fueled when,

office for the reading I was so nervous. My throat was dry. I had a headache and felt I'd never remember the lines. I played my scene on the floor, lying on my back, since there was no couch in the room and I didn't want to play the scene standing. After I finished, I asked if I could do the scene again. Mr. Huston said it wasn't necessary, but I insisted, and he let me do it once more.

When I finished the scene, he turned to me and said, "I don't know why you had to do that scene again. You had the part the first time. But I suppose you had no way of knowing that." And for the first time he smiled at me. He's a genius, that man. He would let me do the scene my way and then tell me what to do to improve the scene.

The star of the film was Louis Calhern, and when the movie was released in 1950 I didn't even appear in the screen credits. But later on, when the film was rereleased, guess what? They gave me star billing!

This was the biggest role I had then on the screen. I was finally out of the sixty-second scenes of my previous pictures. This was my fourth motion picture, and I had a feeling now with more hard work maybe I was finding my way out of the forest.

I was still not under contract to any studio. No studio was interested enough to want to sign me until that great director and writer Joseph Mankiewicz, on the strength

according to Marilyn, she had rejected a pass Crawford had made while visiting Marilyn's home.)

Since Sidney had never bothered to learn to drive, Marilyn often drove him to studio appointments for interviews with the stars, which seemed little enough to do for him. It became a standard laugh at Schwab's to hear this deadpan announcement on the public address system:

"Your chauffeur is here, Mr. Skolsky."

Marilyn repaid Skolsky in yet another way for his availability and boosterism with exclusive stories about her life, and he in turn never printed anything she told him in confidence. Their attachment became so strong that Marilyn would not sign a contract or take part in a movie unless she first spoke with Sidney about it. She became close to Skolsky's wife and daughter, too,

of my role in Asphalt Jungle, signed me for the part of the blonde called Miss Caswell in the picture All About Eve. This role was similar to the one I played in Asphalt Jungle.

I didn't want to do the same thing, so I worked hard at developing the character the way I saw it. I had two scenes in the movie, and I had to play them with George Sanders, the film's male star. Miss Caswell was a dumb blonde, and, though the part was a small one, when Darryl Zanuck viewed the first day's rushes he immediately offered me a contract. I was once again back at Twentieth Century-Fox studios. I began to feel—with such great men as John Huston and Joseph Mankiewicz offering me roles, and with Darryl Zanuck's confidence in me—I just had to work harder and harder to show others that I really wanted to be considered a serious actress.

Maybe now the studio would find the right roles for me. But once again, I was under contract and nothing was happening. They weren't putting me into pictures. What was going to happen to my career as an actress? But that's another story I'll tell you later on.

and the Skolskys became her surrogate family. A rare Hollywood friendship indeed.

Lee Strasberg of the Actors Studio, her mentor and coach on the East Coast, was yet another father figure for Marilyn. She loved the Actors Studio and was excited about the private lessons she took there. Strasberg thought that, if Marilyn worked hard, she could perform credibly on the Broadway stage. She once told me that he, like Skolsky out west, had seen in her a raw but rare talent that if properly and carefully nurtured could produce a great actress. She badly wanted to deserve the faith of men like Strasberg and Skolsky.

Skolsky eventually became a film producer. Among his projects were *The Eddie Cantor Story* and *The Al Jolson Story,* and he hoped to produce *The Marilyn Monroe Story,* but the project was never realized.

11

MARILYN'S CAREER TAKES OFF

*R*emember when I told you about my being back at Fox and nothing was happening for me? Well, one day Roy Croft in the publicity department got a bright idea. He was going to build me up as a pinup, a sex queen. That really did the trick. Editors around the world began publishing my pinup pictures.

The studio began receiving thousands of letters from fans wanting to know who Marilyn Monroe was and wanting a picture of me. The studio said I was receiving more mail for photo requests than their biggest star, Betty Grable. Mr. Zanuck wanted to know just what was going on.

I remember when the studio gave a party for visiting exhibitors. They kept asking me what picture I was going to appear in. I told them they *would have to ask Mr. Zanuck. Even Mr. Spyros Skouras, who was the president of Twentieth Century-Fox, asked me the same question. Everyone wanted to know what my next picture was going to be. Can you imagine how the other studio executives felt when Mr. Skouras said, "The exhibitors and the public like her, so what picture is she in?"*

My contract was soon to expire. The next day the studio entered into negotiations with my agency on a new contract for me. The new contract was for seven years— starting date May 11, 1951, at a salary of five hundred dollars a week, with semiannual raises of two hundred fifty dollars a week additional until the full amount of the contract. I was now twenty-five years old. Then orders were issued by Mr. Zanuck to all producers to find a part for me in their films.

You see, it was my fans who wanted me, who made me a star. The studio was finally doing something about it because of the pressure that came from the public. The signal was given, and I began to appear in one film after another. They put me into a film called As Young as You Feel, *with Monty Woolley. Then came* Love Nest, *with June Haver. In this film I played [a member of] the Womens Army Corps. Then there was* Let's Make It Legal, *with Claudette Colbert and Macdonald Carey. Wow, I was*

GEORGE BARRIS: When Marilyn married Joe DiMaggio, she was in love not only with him, but with his large and loving family, too. She probably found in them, as in the families of other friends and lovers, a replacement for the whole family she had so needed as a young girl. She became especially fond of Joe's son, Joe Jr., and she kept in touch with him even after her divorce from his father. Later on, she remained in contact with Arthur Miller's son and daughter after she and their father had called it quits, and she kept up a friendly relationship with Miller's father as well.

Marilyn's storybook marriage to the American sports icon Joe DiMaggio was doomed from the start; her career demanded that she remain in the public eye; he was through with all that, never liked it much in the first place, and considered

kept busy—I could hardly catch my breath. It was exciting. I was now appearing on the screen regularly.

Then when Mr. Zanuck said, "Miss Monroe is the most exciting new personality in Hollywood in a long time," I tried that much harder to live up to his and my fans' confidence in me. I worked day and night, now more so, to prove that I wanted to be a serious dramatic actress—even though some of the roles I was put in you could hardly believe it at the time.

But I tried very hard at my profession of acting. It was always very important to me not to let my public down. I have an obligation to them. They are the ones who gave me the opportunity, and they still are the people that can make an actress a star.

A few weeks before my marriage to Joe DiMaggio, I was put on suspension by [Fox] for refusing to make a film called The Girl in Pink Tights. It was a remake of an old Betty Grable film. Frank Sinatra was to star with me in it, but I thought the studio could find a more suitable story for me than a remake.

But then when [Joe and I] were married, the studio as a wedding present took me

himself well out of the limelight. He wanted to settle down and make a home. Although Marilyn, too, was basically a private person (she liked more than anything to stay at home and read a book or listen to her favorite Judy Garland and Frank Sinatra recordings), her career was going into overdrive, and there were more and more invitations and appearances that she couldn't afford to turn down if she wanted her fortunes to continue to rise.

A friend of mine, the excellent photographer and producer Sam Shaw, came up with the inspired suggestion for the skirt-blowing scene in *The Seven Year Itch,* a scene that Marilyn has "credited" with being the final cause of the breakup of her marriage to the jealous Joe D. But if Marilyn had wanted to preserve her marriage, she would have had to give up the stardom she had

off suspension and that following summer started another film for me: There's No Business Like Show Business.

We rented a lovely cottage in Beverly Hills and settled down to married life. Everything went fine for a while, until Joe started complaining about my working all the time. He even would find little things to upset him after a while. It got so that we didn't even talk to each other for days. I began living in one part of the house and Joe the other. It was now too much to take. When I did the film The Seven Year Itch, he said my dress-flying scene, my exposing my legs and thighs, even my crotch—that was the last straw.

It was always very important to me not to let my public down.

worked so hard to gain, just when she had finally and fully claimed it.

When I asked questions about her three marriages, Marilyn gave me polite but terse answers. There had been too many bad elements in her relationships with Dougherty, DiMaggio, and playwright Arthur Miller, and these were too intimate to be part of our discussions. She had loved them as best she could, but she had probably never been in love with any of them. She did mention to me some of her memories of the good times, and she was always respectful in talking of the men in her life whom she had married when she was too young, too confused, and too lonely to undertake such a lasting commitment.

12

"AT FIRST, IT ALL WAS INNOCENT AND FUN"

Who would ever dream that my marriage to my second husband, the world-famous former New York Yankees star baseball player Joe DiMaggio, would end in divorce after only nine months? That would have been enough time for us to have a baby, but that never happened. I would never have imagined instead, [that] while I was in New York City on location filming The Seven Year Itch, a scene in the film would be the cause of our breakup.

The year was 1954 and I was busier than ever before. [After] There's No Business Like Show Business was finished that summer, I'd gone into shooting The Seven Year Itch. Sam Shaw, a world-famous photographer-producer and friend of the director, had an idea for a scene. He approached the producer, Charles Feldman, who agreed the idea would be sensational—giving great publicity and zest to the movie. Feldman discussed it with director Billy Wilder, George Axelrod, the screenwriter, and me. We all said, "Let's do it!"

The scene was for Tom Ewell and me to come out of the Trans-Lux movie house on Lexington Avenue. This was a night scene. It was a warm September evening, and we stopped on a subway grating; when a train would pass by, the air could cool me off.

I was wearing a sheer-white, billowy sleeveless dress. When the subway train roared by, it would send up a blast of cool air. There was a subway grating there all right, but everything else was make-believe. No train passing by, but air blowing up was done by the special-effects people stationed underground with a wind-blower machine. This sent my dress flying waist high, revealing my legs and white panties. A crowd had gathered even though it was two or three in the morning. They consisted mostly of men who somehow had heard about our late night-filming. Among the crowd was my husband,

GEORGE BARRIS: When Marilyn Monroe became the world's most famous movie star, she was very suspicious of the invitations she received from presidents, royalty, and important men from all walks of life. Did these men want her company because she interested them or because her presence would bolster their position or their ego? She often sat at home alone at night once she was so much in demand, finding it more to her taste to listen to the music that she enjoyed—besides Garland and Sinatra, she liked Ella Fitzgerald and Mel Torme. She played Garland's "Who Cares" constantly, and Sinatra's version of "That's Why the Lady Is a Tramp" was another favorite.

Despite her fame, when Marilyn was in New York, she could, with the aid of a wig and a kerchief, stroll along the sidewalks of the city unrecognized. That delighted her-Cabbies would whistle at her; other guys would try to pick her up, just as they tried to pick up any other pretty girl out for a stroll. Broadway and the bright lights, the plays—all were there. She could go out as often as she wished and never tired of doing so. She would dream of performing on Broadway in a hit musical or drama. Any opening that she attended was sure to be especially well attended by the press, and the

Joe, and his famous friend, Broadway columnist Walter Winchell. At first, it all was innocent and fun, but when Billy Wilder kept shooting the scene over and over, the crowd of men kept on applauding and shouting, "More, more, Marilyn—let's see more." Joe became upset, especially when the director's camera kept coming in, focusing only on my vagina. Luckily I had been wearing two pairs of panties, hoping no pubic hair would show through. The whistles and the yelling from the male audience became too much for my husband. It was like a burlesque show. What was to be a fun scene turned into a sex scene, and Joe, angry as could be, turned to Winchell, shouting, "I've had it!" And the two men took off.

I turned to Wilder and said, "I hope all these extra takes are not for your Hollywood friends to enjoy at a private party." I couldn't imagine them showing such a scene, especially such a close-up of my private area, in a comedy film made for the family audience.

I was right. When we returned to Hollywood the scene was reshot at the studio in a

photographers could not seem to get enough pictures of her. It often seemed that Marilyn was the star of the play—not just another visitor from Hollywood.

Marilyn had great love for the arts—acting, dancing, music, poetry, and literature. She had once enrolled in the University of Southern California at Los Angeles to improve her limited academic education, but she did not graduate—and she once said that not graduating was her one big regret in life. But she was street smart and she read widely.

★ ★ ★

While Marilyn was still married to Arthur Miller, the couple went to see *An Evening With Yves Montand* on Broadway. After the show, she pronounced its star sexy and said, "When he sings, he moves his body in the most erotic way. He's wonderful!" Although she'd never met Montand or his wife, Simone Signoret, the Millers went backstage and invited Yves and Simone to have supper.

Marilyn soon found out all about Yves. He had been born in Italy, grown up in Marseilles, and had always wanted to be a singer. He'd at first sung in small clubs, and his career didn't take off until he was dis-

more refined way. But Sam Shaw's idea was a great publicity stunt for the film. The photo of my dress flying sky-high up to my panties made every newspaper, every magazine in the world. For the film's premiere showing at New York's Loew's State Theater, its four-story building façade was covered by a huge artist's rendition of that famous dress-blowing scene.

Only two good things came out of that [scene]: one was making friends with [George Barris] when he came to interview and photograph me for the weekly papers; the other was the success of the film. But [as I said before] that dress-flying (or sex) scene was the straw that broke the camel's back. Joe admitted he still loved me but my being a movie star was too much for him to take any longer. He became impossible to live with. I guess at the time there was nothing to do but get divorced.

[On October 6, 1954] I stepped out of our Beverly Hills rented home to give a press interview on the lawn, with tears streaming down my cheeks and a lump in my throat. I held on to my attorney for support and said, "Joe and I are getting a divorce."

Meanwhile in the house [Joe] was packing his belongings. He left the house and put his suitcases in his car while the reporters asked him, "Where you headed, Joe?" He got in his car and shouted, "Going home." Without another word he roared off to San Francisco.

---

covered by the great *chanteuse* Edith Piaf. When Marilyn discovered him, she was slated to make the musical *Let's Make Love* with Gregory Peck. When Peck pulled out, Marilyn knew she had the perfect replacement: Yves Montand.

During the filming the couples lived in adjacent bungalows at the Beverly Hills Hotel. Marilyn and Yves became lovers both off and on the screen. Yves considered her just another of his conquests, but Marilyn was serious about him; she wanted him to leave his wife, and she was willing to leave Arthur. Simone and Arthur seemed to accept their spouses' romance as just one of those things—and probably a temporary one. Sure enough, when the filming was over, so was the romance, as far as Yves was concerned. He rushed back to France and Simone. But Marilyn never got over him.

I wanted a husband, and [I wanted] my career. I guess no husband wants to live in the shadow of his wife's fame. [Later] my marriage to Arthur Miller fell apart. No one wants to be known as "Mr. Marilyn Monroe."

At the completion of The Seven Year Itch, I went to New York and formed Marilyn Monroe Productions, in partnership with magazine photographer Milton H. Greene. For our company I produced a picture in England with Sir Laurence Olivier called The Prince and the Showgirl.

About Sir Laurence: I think Larry at his best is a great actor. It's what you get up there on the screen—he was my choice [as the lead] because I felt there was something incongruous and it would make it interesting. But frankly, he wasn't my choice as a director—but he wanted to direct. Some have told me the film was not a financial success, but I am sure they're wrong. It sure made money; why, I'm making money. It's still making money. I've refused to sell it to television.

She had another serious romance after she and Miller split up—this time she was involved with the president of the United States. In romancing a famous star, John F. Kennedy was following in the footsteps of his father, Joseph P. Kennedy, who had once brazenly taken Gloria Swanson as his mistress. Marilyn was invited to sing "Happy Birthday" at JFK's birthday party in Madison Square Garden in New York City. The president's wife had not been invited, and Marilyn had a Cinderella fantasy that Kennedy would divorce Jackie and marry her, that she would then become first lady. Instead, it is rumored, the president passed her on to his kid brother, Bobby, and after a while this romance soured, too. She never forgave the Kennedy brothers, feeling she had been just another of their rich boy's playthings.

13

"I'M THIRTY-SIX YEARS OLD. I'M JUST GETTING STARTED."

*O*n the film Something's Got to Give I tried to cooperate. I did everything George Cukor, the director, asked of me. When it came to the pool scene, George said it would be more realistic if I would do the swimming-pool scene in the nude, discarding the flesh-skin bathing suit I was to wear.

I agreed to do the swimming-pool scene nude when I was told it would make the film more of a success artistically and commercially. I had never done a nude scene in a motion picture before. I knew the studio was in financial straits because of the Elizabeth Taylor–Cleopatra filming in Rome.

I wanted our picture to be a great one, believe me. I really wanted it to be great. Then I got sick, and, well, you know the rest of the story. The newspapers and magazines have been full of what happened, and now I'm waiting. Everything they've been saying in the press about me is not true. I hope I can continue Something's Got to Give. It can be successful—I know it can, and so does everyone else connected with it. But all I can do is wait until they let me know. I'm ready. I want to work. Acting is my life. I've never felt better. I am not a victim of emotional conflicts. I am human. We all have our areas. We all feel a little inferior, but who ever admits it? I do think I'm human. I do have my down moments, but I'm also robust more than down.

My friends have told me that my ex, Joe, is still in love with me. Well, I still love him, too, but he does have a tendency to be a little hotheaded. It usually does take two to make it work, now, doesn't it?

Let's be fair, I feel friendly toward all my ex-husbands. My advice to couples having marriage problems is, If you're already married, try to save it. If it's impossible, don't try too long. I'm very proud of the fact that I've become friends with my ex-

GEORGE BARRIS: There were many significant people in Marilyn's life. Some of them were good friends, some only acquaintances. She depended heavily upon some of them, and some depended upon her. Some influenced her professionally and intellectually, and a few of them she would have been better off not knowing at all. Here's a Who's Who in the Life of Marilyn Monroe

(For the purposes of this list, a *confidant* or *confidante* is a person to whom secrets are confided.)

Jack Benny, early television star, responsible for her first TV appearance
Irving Berlin, songwriter, friend
Marlon Brando, lover, then close friend
Cyd Charisse, actress, dancer, friend
Montgomery Clift, actor, close friend, she helped his career
Wally Cox, actor, comedian, friend
Joan Crawford, actress, acquaintance, no friend
George Cukor, director, no friend, user
Tony Curtis, actor, acquaintance, no friend

husbands' children. Joe's son, Joe Jr., visited me when he graduated from Marine boot training in San Diego.

I was so proud of Joey when I heard he graduated first in his class. He looked handsome in his Marine uniform, too. I don't want to be a mother to my ex's children—they have a mother. I just would like to remain the good friends that we are.

I'm also proud of the fact that Arthur's father, Isadore Miller, who is in his late eighties, and I have become such good friends. We write and see each other; he's a wonderful man.

As you know, I've never been a nightclubber. When I work I never go out. When I'm not working is when I do go out—usually to friends' house parties, or just [to visit] friends in their homes. We just sit around, have a few drinks, something to eat, listen to good music, and just relax.

Personally I think the best performance I ever gave was in The Asphalt Jungle. Others think Bus Stop, while others say Some Like It Hot. Others The Seven-Year Itch. The worst part I had to play was Let's Make Love—I didn't even have a part. It

---

André de Dienes, photographer, close friend

Joe DiMaggio, baseball legend, husband, friend

Joe DiMaggio Jr., Joe's son, friend

Jim Dougherty, first husband

Ella Fitzgerald, a favorite singer, friend

Agnes Flanagan, hair stylist, early days, close friend to the end

Connie Francis, acquaintance

Clark Gable, actor, last costar, close friend

Milton Greene, photographer, business partner, close friend

Jim Haspel, teenager, top fan, friend

Ben Hecht, author, friend

Johnny Hyde, superagent, confidant, close friend

John Huston, movie director, questionable friend

John F. Kennedy, United States president, heartbreaker, user

Robert F. Kennedy, United States attorney general, heartbreaker, user

Peter Lawford, Kennedy brother-in-law, friend

was part of an old contract. I had nothing to say. The part of the girl was awful. You just had to rack your brain. There was nothing there, I mean script-wise.

When I think of the future, I think, I'm thirty-six years old. I'm just getting started. I'd like to be a fine actress—comedy, tragedy interspersed. I always wanted to be an actress. I'm interested in horticulture, but I don't think I'd want to be a gardener. I'm interested in all the arts. I'm even interested in people. About my last picture, The Misfits, some people like it, but not me. I was disappointed. The director, John Huston, he sort of fancied himself a writer, and he changed it from the original intention of Arthur Miller. Now, this director also did Asphalt Jungle, but he didn't fool around with the script. I personally preferred the script be left as the writer did it. Mr. Miller at his best is a great writer. Any good script I would do.

It's very difficult for me to go from one picture to another. You know what I mean, from six A.M. to six P.M. I like a breather, and I am thirty-six. But as long as one is alive, one can be vital. But you don't give up until you stop breathing.

You know, I like playing around in the garden. It's sort of fun. All there is is work, and there's love.

Natasha Lytess, drama coach, Svengali, friend

Norman Mailer, author, spurned friend

Dean Martin, actor, close friend

Groucho Marx, comedian, helped get first screen role, acquaintance

Bernice Miracle, half sister, confidante

Arthur Miller, writer, husband

Isadore Miller, Arthur's father, friend

Eunice Murray, housekeeper, user, found Marilyn dead

Pat Newcomb, press agent, confidante

Laurence Oliver, actor, director, user

Otto Preminger, film director, no friend

Ronald Reagan, actor, friend

May Reis, close friend

Henry Rosenfeld, businessman, confidant

Norman Rosten, author, he and family were close friends

Lucille Ryman, career adviser, friend

Joe Schenck, producer, close friend from the early days

Sam Shaw, photographer, producer, friend
Phil Silvers, actor, comedian, friend
Frank Sinatra, lover, friend
Sidney Skolsky, columnist, adviser, close
  confidant
Allan "Whitey" Snyder, makeup man, early
  days, close friend to the end
Gloria Steinem, author, casual acquaintance
Lee Strasberg, drama coach, close confidant
Paula Strasberg, drama coach, Svengali,
  friend

Susan Strasberg, actress, confidante
Eli Wallach, friend
Shelly Winters, actress, once roommate,
  close friend
Darryl Zanuck, Fox studio chief, user, no
  friend

I have a small circle of close friends. I like people, oh sure. But some people because I've succeeded didn't remain friendly, and it was because I was busy working. I worked six days a week. The unions changed that to five days, and I [still] didn't get to socializing. People ask me if I paint or write. You know what I tell them? Oh sure, I can paint. Why, I once painted a whole apartment! On writing? I've written a few poems. I keep them to myself. Oh, they are personal, all about just what I observed.

Those people that have been writing all those lies about me. All I know, it's their problem. Those people, I don't even know [them], or if we have met, it's been brief. Can I take it? Are you kidding? I'm used to it, and [remember] the old saying: "Consider the source."

I want to work. Acting is my life . . . .
I am not a victim of emotional conflicts. I am human.

14

"THE HAPPIEST TIME OF MY LIFE IS NOW"

NOTE: This chapter consists of quotes from my interviews with Marilyn that would have been integrated within the text of our completed book as she and I originally envisioned it. I include them here for the insights I believe they offer into Marilyn's personality and character.

On Marriage and Children: *I'm just mad about men. If only there was someone special—of course I would like to be in love. But for marriage again? It hasn't entered my mind since my last one [to Arthur Miller]. The right man might help. I hate living alone—but I'm doing it.*

The thing I want more than anything else? I want a baby! I want to have children! I used to feel [that] for every child I had, I would adopt another, but I don't think a single person should adopt children. There's no Ma or Pa there.

On Aging: *Women as they grow older should take heart. They've gained in wisdom. They're really silly when they are twenty.*

Carl Sandburg, who's in his eighties—you should see his vitality, what he has contributed. Why, he could play the guitar and sing at three in the morning—I like him very much.

On Food, Fragrance, and Flowers: *I love food as long as it has flavor. It's flavorless food I can't stand. I usually have a steak and a green salad for my dinner, also for breakfast when I'm really hungry. I keep away from pastries—I used to love them, and ice cream, too. I skip all desserts unless it's fruit. I just don't like the taste of pastries. As a kid I did, but now I hate it—and as for candy, I can take it or leave it, usually leave it. But I love champagne—just give me champagne and good food, and I'm in heaven and love. That's what makes the world go round.*

I like different scents of perfume, beside Chanel No. 5.

My favorite flower is the delphinium. Roses, any color, are [among my] favorites, too.

GEORGE BARRIS: It was Friday afternoon, August 3, 1962, around five thirty in New York, when I received a phone call from Marilyn. What a pleasant surprise! She asked me about the magazine story and our book project. I told her both were going well.

"There's so much more I want to tell you for the book. When are you coming back?" she asked.

I told her that we had enough for the book—I just needed to ask her a few more questions about this and that, to fill in certain areas that we hadn't really talked about.

She cut in to tell me excitedly that Jack Benny, on whose show she'd made her first television appearance, wanted her to put together a Las Vegas show with him. Frank Sinatra and Marlon Brando (she'd always wanted to work with him) had called with film offers, and a top producer had offered

On Traveling: *I like getting there, not the actual traveling itself. I've never been to Italy, but I love Italians. Paris I hear is a marvelous place, too—the city of lights. It must be beautiful; I hope someday to go there and all these other exciting places.*

I've traveled to England, Korea, Japan, and Mexico. I've been to Canada, too—when I made the film River of No Return, in 1953. We were on location in the Canadian Rockies and Banff. Did you know I almost drowned in the Bow River, when the icy torrent dragged me downstream? I also tore a ligament in my ankle when I tripped over a rock in the river. They had to put me in a cast for ten days when my ankle swelled badly. Now I can laugh about it, but it wasn't funny then. Imagine, this was my contact with nature—poor little me. A big-city girl, drenched, half drowned, and crippled, crushed by the wilderness. But if you remember the picture, I rode a log raft down the rapids. It sure was beautiful country. Oh, yes, how can I ever forget Canada?

On Television and Movies: *The only time I watch television is for the news program or for a good movie. I'm not what you'd call a TV fan. I was going to do Somerset Maugham's Rain—the Sadie Thompson role. I find it an exciting one, but the deal fell through. I wanted Lee Strasberg, my drama coach, to direct me in it, but*

her a starring role in a Broadway play (something else she'd always dreamed of). Fox wanted her to begin shooting a film with Dean Martin in September.

She told me she was reading two wonderful books: *Captain Newman* and *To Kill a Mockingbird.*

"You've just got to get back here," she said. Her voice sounded like she had just hit the jackpot. She never seemed happier.

I told her I'd try to leave by Monday or the middle of the week at the latest, and that I was very happy for her. I asked about her plans for the weekend, and she said she'd probably just relax, go out to dinner, and then maybe go over to the Lawfords for their regular Saturday night party. Then she said, "Love you—see you Monday or when you get out here."

I said I loved her, too.

Fewer than twenty-four hours after Marilyn's phone call, she was dead. The press told the world she had committed suicide. I will never believe Marilyn took her own life. She had too much to live for. She was excited about this book. She sounded so happy. . . . It remains my belief, though I have no proof, that she was murdered.

NBC wanted an experienced TV director. I think it can be an exciting movie for the big screen—I believe in movies. Everyone should get out of their house once in a while—not just sit around with their socks on.

On Acting and Actors: *When anyone asks me for advice on how to become an actress, the only advice I feel qualified to give is only through my own experience. So here goes: Always be yourself. Retain individuality; listen to the truest part of yourself. Study if you can. Get a good teacher. Believe in yourself. Have confidence, too.*

I have favorite motion-picture stars, like everyone else. You know who mine are? My favorite is Marlon Brando. I mean, really, I believe we'd be an interesting combination. I've said that about Marlon for a long time, but we haven't found the right story. Can you imagine us on the big screen? I hope something happens soon.

Greta Garbo, I've never met her. It really bugs me when I miss one of her films on TV. Oh, if you could only get me to meet her! I've also heard wonderful things about Jeanne Eagels and Laurette Taylor. And the one they called the Blond Bombshell: Jean Harlow. Kay Kendall was a great comedian. She was really talented.

I would have loved working with Gérard Philipe, the handsome French star—his films I've been told were a huge success in France, as were his stage plays. I was told he wanted to make films with me. Oh, what a shame we never got the opportunity. We would have made an interesting team. What a shame. He was so young to die; he was thirty-six. He had been ill and apparently died of a heart attack.

On Marilyn: *Those things the press has been saying about me [are fine] if they want to give the wrong impression. It's as simple as all that. I'm not interested in being a millionaire. The one thing a person wants most in life is usually something basic that*

---

money can't buy. I'm not the girl next door—I'm not a goody-goody—but I think I'm human.

As far as I'm concerned, the happiest time of my life is now. There's a future, and I can't wait to get to it.

It should be interesting.

An Appreciation

THAT SUNDAY IN JUNE 1962 when I rang Marilyn's doorbell for the first time, she appeared in a blue-gray Turkish bathrobe that matched her sparkling blue-gray eyes. She held a half-full glass of champagne that caught the sunlight. Even though the robe was tightly wrapped around her body, it could not conceal those famous curves; clearly she wore nothing underneath. She spelled s-e-x from the top of her golden head to the tips of her toes. She had a peaches-and-cream complexion and a fabulously sexy voice. Here was every man's dream of the sexiest woman in the world. I could hardly believe my eyes—this beautiful creature had turned thirty-six on June 1—it seemed that the older she grew, the younger she looked. The first thing she said to me was, "Hi," and then she offered an open smile and invited me to come in.

I was there because Marilyn had finally found time for us to work on our photoessay for *Cosmopolitan* and make some headway on our long-delayed book project. I was to interview Marilyn at home for our book, and she had suggested I bring along a tape recorder. So, along with the (borrowed) recorder, the most beautiful single rose I could buy, and a bottle of her favorite Dom Perignon, I had rung her doorbell, prepared to tape our exclusive interviews.

Marilyn went into the kitchen to get me a beer, and when she returned, we made ourselves comfortable. It turned out that she had changed her mind about talking on tape. She said it made her nervous; she'd be on guard and not able to speak freely. She thought she could give a more intimate interview if I just took notes—and then later on I could fill in the details of our conversations.

Of course I was disappointed, but what she said made sense to me. I

M.M.

(1)

Q. What Do You Want Most out of Life

M.— I feel I'm just getting started after my age of 36

I want to do comedy, tragedy, intense

About men

I'm just mad about one men If there was something special.

About friends:

I have a small circle of close friends

ity to say
ful work
ust head to
n there was
mean

e liberal

me
was
uestion
themsely
myself
attention
this
+ he
with

began to realize that she was a very smart woman who knew exactly how she wanted to work with me. I was going to play by her rules on our project; she would call all the shots. So I agreed and sat back in her new home, the first she had ever owned, to toast her and our project. She said, "Now that I've turned thirty-six, this is a dream come true for me—my having my own home, my own house. I have an apartment in New York City on Sutton Place, and I'm officially a legal resident of New York, but since pictures are still made in Hollywood, that's where I have to be for work. I decided it was time for me to buy a house, instead of leasing one all the time . . . It's a cute little Mexican-style house with eight rooms, and at least I can say it's mine—but not alone. I have a partner."

When I asked her who that might be, she said, "The bank! I have a mortgage to pay off. There's a six- or eight-foot wall for privacy, and my mailbox has no name on it, but the mailman knows who lives here. I don't know if you noticed there are fourteen red stone squares leading to my front door, where there is a ceramic-tile coat of arms with the motto CURSUM PERFECIO, meaning 'end of my journey.' I hope it's true. What's great, too, is that this house is near the ocean *and* the studio. The address is cute, too: 12305 Fifth Helena Drive, Brentwood. And get this, I'm in a cul-de-sac or, as we call it, a dead-end street. It's small, but I find it rather cozy that way. It's quiet and peaceful—just what I need right now.

"I want to give small dinner parties for my friends where we can relax and have some good times. I live here all alone with my snowball, my little white poodle—he was given to me by my dear old friend Frank Sinatra. I call him Maf. Oh sure, it gets lonesome at times living alone; I'd rather be married and have children and a man to love—but you can't always have everything in life the way you want it. You have to accept what comes your way. I live alone and I hate it!"

This friendly, cordial woman seemed nothing at all like a Hollywood power to reckon with, didn't act the stereotype of the star at home. She made me feel welcome right away. She had just recovered from another of the numerous illnesses that had caused Fox to suspend her from work on *Something's Got to Give,* and I could hear sadness in her voice and see it on her face as she described the many "friends" who had deserted her in this crisis.

Later on, we began our photo sessions in the borrowed house in North Hollywood that would stand in for Marilyn's new Brentwood home. Brentwood was near Beverly Hills and Hollywood, but it could have been a million miles away as far as Marilyn was concerned. Although she would have no doubt preferred to be photographed in her own home, I thought its barely furnished condition made it a bit depressing.

As I took pictures of her in Tim Liemert's lovely home, Marilyn would now and then lapse into a blue mood. She would cover her face with both hands, lower her head for a moment or two, and then, smiling, become her old self again—cheerful and clowning for the camera. But I could see a residual tear or two.

Once she walked out into the garden, with its panoramic view of Los Angeles below. Holding her glass of champagne, she lifted her face to the sun and toasted the city where she'd been born, grown up, and had her successes and her failures.

As we talked on there, Marilyn told me she loved the beach, and when I suggested we take a series of photographs at the Santa Monica beach, she was thrilled. That particular beach brought back memories of her childhood, when she had spent many wonderful days there with her mother and her friends.

In her younger days, Marilyn had often driven along the Pacific Coast Highway, enjoying the sunset or the moon's reflection in the water. She might stop with a boyfriend at a small beachside restaurant, have a late dinner, and dance the night away. She might go down to the beach, kick off her shoes, roll up her slacks, and let the cool water caress her feet as she and her friend walked along the sand in the moonlight. "It was sometimes better than sex," she said.

She had continued to enjoy these nights on the beach, and on such

stops after she'd become a star, she needed to disguise herself in order not to be mobbed by fans. Even though she was most often dressed in a baggy sweater and slacks, with a scarf over her hair and huge sunglasses over her eyes despite the darkness, a fan might come up and ask, "Did anyone ever tell you, you look just like Marilyn Monroe?"

Marilyn would laugh and reply, "All the time."

She wasn't the only Californian who loved the beach—there were plenty of others who often spent whole days there, so finding a quiet, uncrowded area was a problem when we went there, but we finally located a place the other beachgoers had overlooked. The spot was near the old Peter Lawford house, where rumor has it Marilyn had trysted with John Kennedy and later with his brother Bobby. If Marilyn noticed, she didn't say so.

I was surprised by the respect Marilyn's fans showed her during the sessions at Santa Monica beach. No one bothered us; the people who gathered around spoke in whispers.

Of course there were exceptions to the generally respectful treatment by the fans: A very regal lady once paraded majestically into camera range and, with a slow sideways glance, indicated that it would be perfectly okay to include her in a photo or two. On another occasion, a couple of picnickers positioned themselves for a clear view of our work and politely asked anyone blocking their front-row view of the star to please move on. The teenage boys were the funniest—they would mimic Marilyn's sultry poses, much to their own amusement, as well as our own.

But the "mystery lady" intrigued us. Wearing a large straw hat that concealed her face, she stood silently and almost motionless as she watched the goings-on. All of us wondered who this presence might be. Sometime later, when I was visiting Mae West, she revealed that she had been the mystery lady. Although she'd never met Marilyn, the sex queen of years gone by was an admirer of the work of the current sex queen. Mae West said, "Oh, if only I could have met her. It would have been such an honor to talk to her. She's such a beautiful and talented actress."

But the hero of our picture days at the beach was Marilyn herself. Photography is hard work for the photographer but even harder for his model. Both of us wanted every picture to be as exciting, unusual, and yet natural as could be. We worked as a team, and both of us came up with ideas for the pictures. As a former photographer's model, Marilyn was a pro posing for the still camera—and that shows clearly in the pictures I took of her then.

We were both relaxed during our beach shoot, and some of our best photos were taken there. The Santa Monica beach photos were Marilyn's favorites among all those I took of her. They may well have reminded her of the ones that had been taken when she was just nineteen, top model at the Snively agency and dreaming of becoming a star.

The weather during June and July 1962 was often cloudy, with occa-

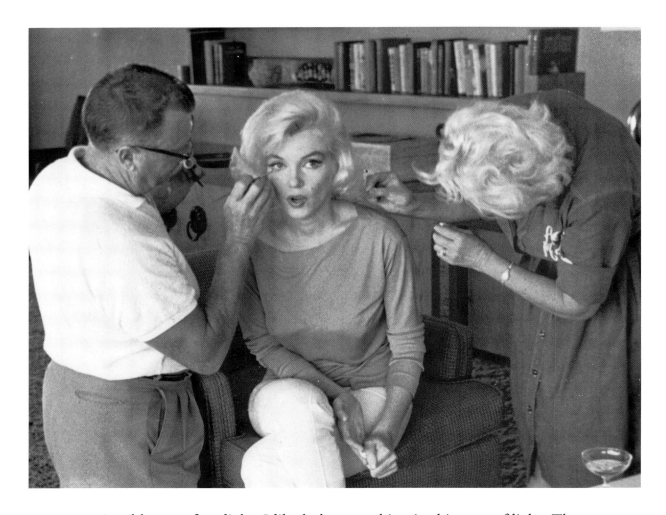

sional bursts of sunlight. I liked photographing in this type of light. The clouds encouraged the soft light I wanted for the moody, reflective experiences I thought appropriate to that time in her life, while the sunlight produced the cheerful days she was to recall in other photos.

Marilyn was often late for our photo sessions. One day I waited for her for what seemed like hours, when suddenly she appeared on the beach with a strange-looking hairdresser and an even stranger-looking makeup man; the car was filled with clothes. I knew she never traveled with an entourage, so these two had to be her faithful friends, Agnes

Flanagan and Allan "Whitey" Snyder, who were constantly at Marilyn's beck and call. (This time she hadn't brought along the third member of her "family," Pat Newcomb, who handled Marilyn's press and acted as her majordomo. She handled Marilyn's wardrobe and her fans, but was much more than an employee; she was a best friend. She was ten years younger than Marilyn, but I couldn't tell the difference in their ages; both looked much younger than they were.)

On this day, the sun had disappeared over the horizon and the sky was turning dark. She looked at me with tears in her eyes. "I'm sorry," she sobbed. "Is there any way you can take the pictures without light?"

How could I get angry at her? There was always an excuse, and I was sure it was legitimate. I gave her a hug and said not to worry, we'd do it another day.

And to prove her sincerity, the next time we worked at the beach she gave more than her all, with never a complaint, never a break. She was determined to make it up to me. Marilyn was a real trooper. Even when the sun went down and the winds blew and it became cold, and she shivered, her skin turned red and her lips blue, she hardly whimpered or complained. Only when the day was almost over and I had just one last bit of film in the camera, she said, "This is for you, George." Then she puckered up her lips and blew a kiss my way as I took the last picture of her ever on that beach. It was around 7:30 P.M., Friday, July 13, 1962.

At the end of that same day I lost one of my shoes when a huge wave came and took it away. I asked her, "What do I do with one shoe?"

"The ocean apparently needs it more than you do," she said, and with that, both of us barefoot, we left Santa Monica beach forever.

When I look at the contact prints of the black-and-white pictures I shot, I remember that Marilyn always checked the photos carefully. Once she said, "Can you make larger prints of those pictures I've marked so I can get a better look at myself?" As a reminder, she even marked those photos she selected on the contact sheet with a red grease pencil.

She would spend hours scrutinizing pictures of herself and, of those she especially liked, she would sometimes loudly remark, "Now, that's really me!" Her experience as a photographer's model had taught her to appreciate how she photographed. She was such a perfectionist that even if only a hair was not in place in a photo she would become upset. "We should have waited for the wind to stop blowing so hard—next time, let's remember this," she might remark.

We were trying to re-create various stages of her life in those pictures. Even in the photographs meant to show her in her adult years. One day I noted that little Norma Jeane appeared in many of them, and I said,

"There always will be the little girl in Marilyn Monroe." Her reply was a broad smile.

She never told me not to print or use any photos of her in our book, in other publications, or in any other way. The markings she made were meant to indicate the pictures that contained no defects. She wanted me to make large prints of those photos for her. She said that those pictures were some of the best and most natural ever taken of her. "That's really me, freckles and all. The real me."

★   ★   ★

When my brother-in-law told me that Marilyn was dead, only days before I was to meet her again in Los Angeles, I broke out in a cold sweat. I felt a pounding in my chest, and for a few seconds I couldn't respond. Then I said, "Come on, Frank, don't make bad jokes. I just spoke to her; I'm going to the coast to see her on Monday." I knew I had to get back to New York City to find out what had happened.

I drove the hundred miles to my Sutton Place apartment at record speed. The doorman said reporters were asking for me. The elevator couldn't get me up to my apartment fast enough. As I opened the door, I could hear the phone ringing. I turned on the radio and television. All the stations were blaring the news of the death of Marilyn Monroe, how it appeared to be a suicide. The press wanted interviews with me; the phone didn't stop ringing. It's not true, I said to myself, I don't believe it. But it was true. We'd last spoken on August 3, 1962, only one day before she died.

★ ★ ★

My phone kept ringing all night long. Friends were calling—more press. I had nothing to say.

Monday morning, after a sleepless night, I went to the office, simply because I couldn't think of anything else to do. It was only eight o'clock when I got there. The office was empty—the staff didn't arrive until ten. I sat at my desk half asleep. The phone rang. It was Stan Mays, the local correspondent for the *London Daily Mirror*. Stan worked out of the *New York Daily News* editorial offices on a reciprocal arrangement. He sounded frantic. He had been trying to locate me and wanted me to come over right away with my interviews and photos of Marilyn. I told Stan I was still working on my *Cosmo* story and the book. I said I'd get back to him, but Stan insisted, "Just get over here as soon as you can."

I finally reached the *Cosmo* editor, Bob Atherton. He said, "Not only is Marilyn dead—so is your story. By the time we come out in November it will be old news. George, your story is now hard news. In respect to

Marilyn, let her story finally be told to her fans and the public, those millions who loved her." I wondered whether Marilyn would want me to tell it. I retrieved my photos and text from *Cosmo* and from my office and then walked the short distance to the *Daily News* to see Stan. I was still in shock, still groggy from a sleepless night.

After looking at the text and photos, Stan immediately picked up his phone and called his editor in London. He whispered into the phone, "I finally tracked George Barris down; his photos and interviews on Marilyn are sensational." The rest of Stan's phone conversation was brief. When he hung up, he said, "The boss wants you to fly out to London right away with your story on Marilyn, all expenses paid, to negotiate exclusive one-time British rights."

Before I quite realized what was happening, I was on a plane to London. When I arrived, a limousine was waiting for me at Heathrow, London's main airport. It was early Tuesday morning as we sped off to the London Daily Mirror Building, escorted by three burly reporters. I was told later they were there to guard me from being kidnapped by the competition, a newspaper called *News of the World,* that was desperately seeking my story. That seemed like something from a James Bond movie, but, then again, in London anything is possible.

The *London Daily Mirror* editor (I never did get his name) assured me he was mainly interested in my photos of Marilyn, since his paper was one that featured photos and few words. The story he wanted was to be about my working with Marilyn in those last days. I asked him not to sensationalize the story, and he promised not to use more than a dozen photos. He kept his word and played it straight.

I had spent less than an hour in the *Mirror* office, yet the editor assigned his top feature writer, Tony Miles, to accompany me to Los Angeles. Marilyn's funeral was to be the next day, Wednesday, August 8, and the editor promised I would be back in time.

It was still Tuesday morning when we left. I had been in London less than three hours when our plane departed for Los Angeles via New

York. Tony was assigned for further interviews with me since the *Mirror* planned to run the Marilyn story over several days.

Our plane arrived in New York late Tuesday evening. There were no direct flights from London to Los Angeles in those days. With a change of planes we arrived in Los Angeles around three Wednesday morning, just enough time to check into the Beverly Wilshire Hotel and catch a few hours of needed rest. I left the hotel around noon to attend Marilyn's funeral at the Westwood Memorial Park. It was a short limousine ride, but when I got there the services had already started and the chapel door was closed. I could not enter.

As I waited outside for the services to end, some members of the press noticed me, one reporter yelling, "Hey, George, how come the special treatment?" The press was roped off from the chapel and the crypt, Marilyn's final resting place. I walked over to the reporters and replied quietly, "I'm here as a friend of Marilyn's—see, no notebook, no camera."

After the services I followed the funeral procession the short distance to the crypt, where Marilyn was to be laid to rest. Joe DiMaggio, her second husband, had made the plans for Marilyn's funeral but invited only a few close friends. Her first and third husbands were not there.

DiMaggio had decided not to invite the Hollywood crowd of movie stars. When Sammy Davis Jr., Frank Sinatra, and many other celebrities tried to attend, they were refused entry. They loved Marilyn and could not understand DiMaggio's attitude. But Joe blamed them for Marilyn's death, thinking them responsible for her careless lifestyle.

At the crypt prayers were said for Marilyn with tears and sobs from the mourners. Noticeably absent was Marilyn's mother, Gladys, who was under the care of Marilyn's half sister, Bernice Miracle, and remained in Florida because of her mental condition. When Gladys learned of Marilyn's death, she said, "I never wanted her to become an actress."

When I returned to the hotel after the services for Marilyn, I found a phone message from the editor of the *New York Daily News*. He wanted me to call him as soon as I could. He asked that I return to New York City as soon as possible. He wanted my Marilyn story and was upset that I was in his editorial offices, right under his nose, and the *London Daily Mirror* had beaten him to the punch. "Wait until I get my hands on Stan Mays," he shouted into the phone.

Tony Miles and I caught the afternoon flight for New York. We were met at New York's La Guardia airport by a team of *Daily News* reporters who wisked us off in a limo to the New Weston Hotel on 48th Street between Madison Avenue and Fifth Avenue. We were kept away from the *Daily News* so that the competition could not get my story. Again, I was reminded of a scene from the famous Broadway play *The Front Page,* in which newspaper competition for a front-page story had reporters hiding their source from their competitors.

The *News* assigned Theo Wilson, their top byline feature reporter, to the Marilyn story. Like the *London Daily Mirror,* the *Daily News* emphasizes photos in its stories.

The *London Daily Mirror* series started Wednesday, August 8, 1962, and ran for four days. The New York *Daily News* story began on Tuesday, August 14, 1962, and ran for a full week. Each newspaper had the largest circulation in its country; yet only ten percent of my text interviews with Marilyn Monroe appeared in these stories and only a dozen photos were used.

During August 1972, a photo exhibition called "The Legend and the Truth" was held at the David Stuart gallery on La Cienega Boulevard in Los Angeles. The exhibition consisted of photographs of Marilyn taken by a dozen topflight photographers, including myself. The exhibit was a huge success; *Life* magazine did a cover story with an eight-page spread. Many book publishers became interested, and that same year Grosset and Dunlap published a book based on the exhibit and titled *Marilyn,* with a text by Pulitzer Prize–winning author Norman Mailer. The book featured photographs by twenty-four of the world's foremost photographers and was produced by Larry Schiller, one of those photographers. Only ten of my photos appeared in that book (five in color and five in black and white). No text of mine or Marilyn's appeared there.

The book instantly became a worldwide bestseller. The publisher's editor in chief (and vice president), Bob Markel, later became my agent. Norman Mailer had never met Marilyn, and his text consisted of his impressions of Marilyn combined with the impressions of others. Mailer, a friend of Marilyn's former husband, Arthur Miller, had asked Miller to introduce him to her several times. Marilyn had refused to meet him. She just didn't like his style.

In 1965 Richard Seaver, president and editor of Henry Holt and Company, was eager to publish a book about Marilyn Monroe from a woman's point of view. Seaver hoped to interest a writer in explaining Marilyn as an individual and as an icon. Gloria Steinem, cofounder of *Ms.* magazine and a leader in the women's liberation movement, and I were brought together by Seaver. His idea was to use some of my pictures of Marilyn (and some by other photographers') and to have Gloria explore the viewpoints of women influenced by Marilyn, to identify who those women were and how they've become important, and ultimately to indicate how Marilyn was ahead of the women of her day.

Steinem, Seaver, and I agreed to create a special fund to help children in need, including those who are emotionally disturbed. Steinem's fee as a writer and a portion of my royalties and the publisher's profits were to make up the initial fund. Readers were invited to contribute, too.

The Steinem book, called, *Marilyn—Norma Jeane,* was published in

1986 and made the *New York Times* bestseller list. It contained eighty-two of my photos of Marilyn (fifty-five in black and white and twenty-seven in color). Steinem used brief quotes from my last interviews with Marilyn, along with many other sources. (Steinem herself had once briefly encountered Marilyn at the Actors Studio in New York.)

★　★　★

Compiling this edition of *Marilyn* has brought back many memories, both happy and sad. I hope that the spirit that I think shines through in these photographs of a complex and delightful woman will bring memories and joy to the readers of this book.

Marilyn Monroe's Films

In my conversations, interviews, and talks with Marilyn, I often wondered how in her fourteen years of filmmaking she would have remembered all the roles she played and what she thought of them.

I had in mind to make a list of her films, and if there were any critic's reviews of her roles to discuss them with her, and I did discuss some of her films with Marilyn. While others have written that Marilyn appeared in twenty-nine films, here is my list—which shows she appeared in thirty motion pictures.

1. **Dangerous Years,**
   Twentieth Century-Fox, 1947
   Plays a waitress

2. **Scudda-Hoo! Scudda-Hay!,**
   Twentieth Century-Fox, 1948
   She appears in a brief scene only

3. **Ladies of the Chorus,**
   Columbia Pictures, 1948
   "Marilyn's singing is one of the brightest spots in the film. She is pretty and with her pleasant voice and style she shows promise."
   —Tibor Krekes
   Motion Picture Herald

4. **Love Happy,**
   United Artist, Pickford, 1950
   Walk-on; two speaking lines. No review, no film credit

5. **A Ticket to Tomahawk,**
   Twentieth Century-Fox, 1950
   Her first singing role, no review

6. **The Asphalt Jungle,**
   Metro-Goldwyn-Mayer, 1950
   "There's a beautiful blonde name of Marilyn Monroe who makes most of her footage."
   —Liza Wilson
   Photoplay

7. **All About Eve,**
   Twentieth Century-Fox, 1950
   Small, convincing role

8. **The Fireball,**
   Twentieth Century-Fox, Thor, 1950

9. **Right Cross,**
Metro-Goldwyn-Mayer, 1950
Bit part, no credits

10. **Home Town Story,**
Metro-Goldwyn-Mayer, 1951
Bit part

11. **As Young as You Feel,**
Twentieth Century-Fox, 1951
"Marilyn Monroe superb as secretary."
—Bosley Crowther
New York Times

12. **Love Nest,**
Twentieth Century-Fox, 1951
Gets bigger roles.

13. **Let's Make It Legal,**
Twentieth Century-Fox, 1951
Brief role as a beautiful, shapely blonde.
"Marilyn amusing."
—Wanda Hale
New York News

14. **Clash by Night,**
RKO, Wald-Krasna, 1952
"The new blonde bombshell."
—Kate Cameron
New York News

15. **We're Not Married,**
Twentieth Century-Fox, 1952
"Marilyn supplies beauty. She is
Hollywood's foremost expert."
—Alton Cook
New York World-Telegram

16. **Don't Bother to Knock,**
Twentieth Century-Fox, 1952
"She is what movies need."
—Frank Quinn
New York Daily Mirror

17. **Monkey Business,**
Twentieth Century-Fox, 1952
"Not seen her before, I know now what
that's about."
—Paul C. Beckley
New York Herald Tribune

18. **O. Henry's Full House,**
Twentieth Century-Fox, 1952
"Again as sleek as in *Asphalt Jungle,*
Marilyn Monroe is a streetwalker of
stunning proportions."
—Archer Winston
New York Post

19. **Niagara,**
Twentieth Century-Fox, 1953
"Seen from any angle, Niagara Falls and
Marilyn Monroe leave little to be desired.
She can be seductive even when she
walks."
—A. H. Weiler
New York Times

20. **Gentlemen Prefer Blondes,**
Twentieth Century-Fox, 1953
"As usual she looks as though she'd glow
in the dark, and her version as the baby-
face blonde whose eyes open for diamonds
and close for kisses is always amusing. as
well as alluring."
—Otis L. Guernsey
New York Herald Tribune

21. How to Marry a Millionaire,
Twentieth Century-Fox, 1953
"Her magnificent proportions are appealing as ever, her stint as a deadpan comedienne is as nifty as her looks."
—Otis L. Guernsey
New York Herald Tribune

22. River of No Return,
Twentieth Century-Fox, 1954
"There is something at once incongruous and strangely stimulating in her dazzled and dazzling antics in the surrounding nature."
—Archer Winston
New York Post

23. There's No Business Like Show Business,
Twentieth Century-Fox, 1954
"Marilyn's songs, performed in her trademark sexy manner, are sizzling."
—Frank Quinn
New York Daily Mirror

24. The Seven Year Itch,
Twentieth Century-Fox, 1955
"Marilyn Monroe clearly plays the role. . . . Tom Ewell steals the picture, but this isn't to detract from her status as a film comedienne."
—Bosley Crowther
New York Times

25. Bus Stop,
Twentieth Century-Fox, 1956
"Hold on to your chairs, get set for a rattling surprise, Marilyn Monroe has

finally proved herself an actress. She and picture are swell!"
—Bosley Crowther
New York Times

26. The Prince and the Showgirl,
Warner Bros., 1957
"Marilyn Monroe has never seemed more in command. She manages to make her laughs without sacrificing the real Marilyn to playacting. This is something one can expect from great talent."
—Archer Winston
New York Post

27. Some Like It Hot,
United Artists, Mirish, 1959
"She's a comedienne with that combination of sex appeal and timing that just can't be beat."
—Haft
Variety

28. Let's Make Love,
Twentieth Century-Fox, 1960
"Marilyn basically is a first-rate comedienne. She doesn't have a single bright line. The famous charms are in evidence."
—Justin Gilbert
New York Mirror

29. The Misfits
United Artists, Seven Arts, John Huston Production, 1961
"Clark Gable has never done anything better. Gable's acting vibrant, lusty;

[Monroe's] true to the character by Miller."
—Kate Cameron
New York Daily News

30. **Something's Got to Give**
(uncompleted),
Twentieth Century-Fox, 1991
Fox TV, 2-hour film; theatrical release overseas
Henry Schipper at Fox contacted me in November 1990. He said he was going to produce Marilyn's last film as a "Tribute to a Star." He wanted to use my last photos of Marilyn as the ending to his film. I told him I would not be interested, since it was at Twentieth Century-Fox that all her problems occurred during her last days—and I couldn't forget that. After several weeks of pleading calls from him, I finally agreed to allow him to use one of my final color photos of her standing on the beach and holding a glass of champagne.